The Complete Guide to

Hamster Care and Ownership

Rianne Bruty

Publication Data
Rianne Bruty
The Complete Guide to Hamster Care and Ownership – First edition.
Summary: "Successfully caring for and owning a hamster"
Provided by publisher.
ISBN: 978-1-954288-93-5
[1. The Complete Guide to Hamster Care and Ownership – Non-Fiction] I. Title.

This book has been written with the published intent to provide accurate and authoritative information in regard to the subject matter included. While every reasonable precaution has been taken in preparation of this book the author and publisher expressly disclaim responsibility for any errors, omissions, or adverse effects arising from the use or application of the information contained inside. The techniques and suggestions are to be used at the reader's discretion and are not to be considered a substitute for professional veterinary care. If you suspect a medical problem with your hamster, consult your veterinarian.

Design by Sorin Rădulescu
First paperback edition, 2023

TABLE OF CONTENTS

Chapter 9

Conclusion

CHAPTER 1

Introduction to Hamsters

Since the 1930s, hamsters have been tamed and kept as pets due to their cute appearance and friendly nature. Over the last 100 years, hamsters have become the most common rodent for children to have as pets. They're the third most common children's pet, second only to dogs and cats.

FUN FACT

The word hamster comes from "hamstern," a German term for stockpiling or hoarding, which refers to the hamster's habit of stashing food in pouches located inside its mouth.

Why are hamsters so popular with kids? It might be because of their super-soft fur or their beady little eyes or their twitchy noses or maybe their cheeky personalities. Or perhaps it's because a hamster is often the first pet that doesn't belong to the whole family but is a child's very own!

Unlike cats and dogs, hamsters don't require a great deal of space for their housing, nor are they costly to maintain. They're naturally tidy creatures that organize their habitats so that they have a separate sleeping area, eating area, and bathroom. Several species are naturally friendly, and they enjoy being held and gently played with. In time, Syrian hamsters are able to recognize their name and their owner. A hamster could be just the companion you're looking for!

Hamsters can be a great choice for a pet, especially for a child, but, like any living creature, they require the right food, a source of clean water, a safe home, mental stimulation, and physical activity.

FUN FACT
Internet Hamster Association of North America (IHANA)

The Internet Hamster Association of North America (IHANA) is an online resource for hamster enthusiasts and breeders. This digital club lists affiliated breeders, hamster standards according to the British Hamster Association (BHA), and links to hamster clubs and associations by region. For more information, visit www.ihana.org.

The History of the Hamster

Nineteen breeds of hamsters have been recognized around the world, although only a handful of these have been domesticated and are kept as pets. Each species of these cute little fluffballs has a unique and colorful history as well as distinctive physical characteristics and behaviors. Every hamster, regardless of where they're purchased, has a wild ancestor that originated in either southeast Europe, the Middle East, or Asia.

Wild hamsters collect food that they bring home and store. They live in a network of underground tunnels and chambers in burrows that are up to a meter deep. In general, they live solitary lives and are fiercely territorial. Many wild hamsters live in warm, dry climates.

Domesticated Hamster Species

There are four species—one of which has two variants—that have been domesticated and are popular pets around the world.

Syrian Hamster

Syrian hamsters, sometimes called "golden" hamsters because of their original straw coloring and their friendly nature, were discovered and first categorized in the late 1700s in the Aleppo region of Syria. They were believed to have become extinct by the 1800s, but then a Syrian mother hamster and her 12 babies were sighted, caught, and brought to the United Kingdom in 1930. It's believed that every domesticated Syrian hamster is descended from that single family of hamsters!

Syrian Hamster

Syrians have evolved to have approximately 40 different fur colors that range from various browns to black to creams and grays. The length of their fur also varies from short hair to long hair with a rex (short and curly) variation. The long-haired Syrian hamster is often referred to as a Teddy Bear hamster.

Chinese Hamster

Chinese hamsters, so called because they were discovered in northern China, are believed to be the descendants of several wild breeds. Although they're smaller

FUN FACT

Male hamsters are called boars, and females are called sows.

than Syrian hamsters, Chinese hamsters aren't considered to be a dwarf species. Also, unlike Syrian hamsters and many other breeds, Chinese hamsters live with their family in the wild, and domesticated Chinese hamsters do well with cage mates—but more on that later. These animals are dark

Chinese Hamster

gray with a darker stripe down the back and a white tummy. Chinese hamsters are extremely active and, therefore, aren't easy to handle. They require large enclosures with plenty of room to run around.

NOTE: Some states, such and California and New Jersey, require a permit to own, breed, or sell Chinese hamsters.

Russian Dwarf Species— the Campbell's Dwarf and the Winter White Dwarf

The Russian dwarf species is similar in color to the Chinese hamster, but Russian hamsters are smaller, fatter, and rounder than their more slender Chinese cousins. Their chubbiness and

Campbell's Dwarf

dense fur make it easier for them to live in the chilly northern Russian climate. However, wild members of this species are more of a brown color than gray.

There are two Russian dwarf species that are commonly kept as pets—the Campbell's Dwarf hamster and the Winter White Dwarf hamster. These two species can interbreed.

The Campbell's Dwarf hamster is named for Charles William Campbell, who was the first to capture a member of this species in Mongolia in 1904. This species comes in a wide variety of colors. Campbell's Dwarfs are active and fun to watch. They can sometimes be kept in small groups in one enclosure, but they tend to be territorial, so the habitat needs to be big enough that each animal has plenty of space. This species is more susceptible to diabetes than other types of hamsters.

Winter White Dwarf

The second domesticated Russian dwarf species is the Winter White Dwarf hamster. These are typically white in captivity, but in the wild, they change color depending on the season. Since they originated in Siberia, it was necessary for their fur to change to white to camouflage them in the snow in winter, and the grays and browns allowed them to blend into the earth at other times of the year. The Winter White Dwarf has a different body shape than its cousin, the Campbell's Dwarf. It's also more docile than the Campbell's Dwarf.

Roborovski Hamster

The final domesticated species, the Roborovski hamster, is the smallest of these animals and is relatively new in terms of being a household pet. Its fur patterns are similar to the Russian dwarf species, with a dark gray stripe down the back. However, their body color is lighter—basically a dove gray. Although "Robos" have the friendliest temperament among the dwarf breeds, because of their size, high energy, and speed, Robos aren't a good choice as a pet for children. Also, these characteristics mean this hamster isn't a great cuddler like the Syrian hamster. It's always on the move, so a Robo is more suited to being observed than handled. Even though Robos are tiny, they require a large enclosure because of their high activity level. They also need a variety of toys to keep them entertained.

Roborovski Hamster

What Does a Hamster Look Like?

Most rodents that are kept as pets have short and sturdy legs, two small ears, two beady eyes, tiny claws, whiskers, and a button nose. So how can you be sure the pet you're buying is a hamster and not something else? You consult the hamster checklist below!

Hamster Checklist:

- **Does the rodent have a short tail?**

If your answer to this question is no, you definitely don't have a hamster and need to return your rodent to wherever you bought it for a refund! Hamster tails are short, so you may not see it at first. The tail of a Syrian hamster looks like a large grain of rice. The tail is hairless and is nested in the animal's fluffy fur. Dwarf hamsters' tails are even smaller than those of Syrian hamsters and are usually white with fine hair. Chinese hamsters are sometimes confused with mice due to their longer tails. Their tails aren't nearly as long as those of a mouse, rat, or gerbil but are definitely longer than the tail of a Syrian hamster. If you're unsure if an animal is a Chinese hamster or a mouse, look at the rodent's other physical characteristics or do an online search for images of both.

- **How big is the rodent?**

Syrian hamsters are the largest variety of hamster. There have been reports of Syrian hamsters that are 12 inches long, but this is unusual. Most domesticated Syrian hamsters are between five and nine inches long. The female of the

FUN FACT
How Many Species?

Although only five species of hamster are commonly kept as pets, there are many more in the wild. Over 20 different species of hamsters exist worldwide, most of which live entirely in the wild and can be found across Europe and Asia. The largest wild hamster is the European black-bellied hamster, which typically measures 8 to 12 inches long as an adult. Unfortunately, these wild European hamsters are now critically endangered.

Photo Courtesy of Kaitlin Boruff

species is often larger than the male. The habitat you provide for your Syrian hamster needs to be spacious enough for a creature of this size, so if you purchase a juvenile Syrian hamster, keep in mind that it will grow.

Chinese hamsters grow to an average of three to five inches in length and are the second largest of the five main species of pet hamsters.

Dwarf Russian and dwarf winter hamsters usually grow to an average of three inches in length, and they don't get a whole lot bigger if they're purchased as juveniles like Syrian hamsters do.

The bodies of hamsters are wider than the longer, sleeker bodies of other rodents, such as mice or gerbils. The body of a Syrian hamster could be compared to the shape of a potato, and dwarf hamsters look like fuzzy golf balls—noticeably different from other rodents!

The smallest of the common hamster species, the Roborovski, is often confused with Russian hamsters due to its similar-colored fur and the darker stripe along its spine. If you were to compare them side by side, you'd notice the lighter color of the Roborovski's fur and its smaller size.

If you find yourself with a rodent the size of a shoe, you might own a world record-sized Syrian hamster. However, it's more likely that you've bought a guinea pig and not a hamster!

- **Does your rodent store food in pouches in its cheeks?**

Hamsters, like chipmunks and other ground squirrels, such as prairie dogs and marmots, store their food in pouches in their mouth. The technical name of these pouches is hamster cheeks (yes, really). This inner cheek extends to the animal's shoulder and is used to temporarily store food and bedding. These cheeks are an evolutionary attribute that enables hamsters to quickly gather and store food when out in the open and then move to safety as soon as possible. In the wild, hamsters are the prey of many birds and woodland animals, such as foxes. Once in the safety of their burrows or bed, they empty their pouches and either store or eat the food they've collected.

Are Hamsters Good Pets?

> *Hamsters can be wonderful first-time pets as they are busy, curious, and adventurous creatures! Hamsters become accustomed to their owner's voice and scent and make positive associations with them, provided they are well cared for. A hamster will surprise you with its clever efforts to problem-solve, and they can be good communicators once you are able to recognize their behavior and cues.*
>
> JESSICA BRESLER
> *Poppy Bee Hamstery*

The Positive Attributes of Hamsters

- **Hamsters are cuddly, friendly, affectionate, and social.**
Syrian and Chinese hamsters are solitary animals, which is unusual for rodents. Dwarf hamsters can occasionally be housed in pairs or groups, but often disagreements arise, and the animals must be separated. It's important to be aware of this so you can plan to have other habitats available or be willing to rehome one or more of your hamsters. For a solitary hamster, you're its only source of socialization, and this gives you the opportunity to forge a real friendship with your pet if you put in the time.

- **Hamsters are relatively low maintenance and easy to care for.**
Yes, hamsters need their habitat cleaned, and they need food and fresh water. They also need entertainment. But this is true of all pets.

Hamsters are able to eat a variety of food and aren't all that fussy about what they're fed. So, for this reason—and because they eat so little relative to a dog, for example—food costs are low. Cleaning their habitat is made easier since hamsters normally choose a corner of their enclosure to use as a toilet. This means you can spot-clean that area daily in between regular cleanings of the habitat.

Potential Negatives/Considerations

- **Hamsters are nocturnal, so they like to sleep during the day.**

This can mean that people who wish to play with their hamster during the day will be harassing an animal that's trying to sleep. This disrupts their natural biorhythm, which isn't healthy for them, plus they may be grumpy and bite if you wake them!

A nocturnal roommate means that just when you're settling down for a quiet night of sleep, your hamster will be waking up and ready for action. It will likely jump into its noisy exercise wheel or rummage through its food bowl. For some people, this can be annoying, so you might consider putting your hamster's habitat somewhere else in the house when you're trying to sleep.

- **Hamsters are fast.**

Given the chance, regardless of whether it's your friend or not, your hamster will make a run for it. This can cause children to panic and grab the animal too tightly when trying to catch it, possibly injuring it. Grabbing the hamster will also cause *it* to panic, and if it becomes too frightened, it can have a heart attack and die. So, to prevent injuring your hamster or

Photo Courtesy of
Finn Alford

worse, your pet should have a safe and secure play space where it can explore and the two of you can have fun.

● **Hamsters have sharp teeth.**

Hamsters have teeth, which means they can bite—you. They also have tiny claws that usually don't cause any real damage to the skin but can occasionally scratch.

Hamsters, unlike humans, are born with their adult teeth. They have 16 teeth in total, but the most noticeable ones are the four incisors in the front—two on the top and two especially long ones on the bottom. These are usually yellowish in color, and they're very sharp. A hamster's only means of defending itself is to bite, which it may do if it feels threatened or frightened.

Even though a hamster is small, its bite is painful and often draws blood. So you need to ask yourself if you're okay with the possibility that your hamster may bite. The smaller the hamster breed, the more likely it is to bite. Biting is fairly common in the dwarf breeds, even if they're handled when young. This is a real consideration when choosing your hamster. Syrian hamsters are the most docile breed, so if you want the best chance of not being bitten, choose a Syrian hamster for a pet.

Chinese hamsters are also a good choice when it comes to an animal that's unlikely to bite.

● **Hamsters' personalities vary among species.**

As mentioned, Syrian hamsters are usually the friendliest of the breeds, followed closely by the Chinese hamster.

Dwarf and Roborovski hamsters wake for periods during the day, which means there are opportunities to watch them play. Roborovski hamsters are good-natured toward humans, making them suitable for younger owners. However, other dwarf hamster species are typically not sociable with humans. They have a tendency to bite and, for that reason, aren't good choices for children.

This is important to note because when dwarf hamsters first became popular as pets, lots of people purchased them, thinking they'd be good companions for both adults and children. It soon became clear that other than Robo hamsters, members of dwarf species generally didn't like to be handled, and biting was common. As a result, many dwarf hamsters were given to hamster-rescue organizations, and those became overrun with dwarf hamsters that were difficult to find homes for because of their unsociability.

If you enjoy watching hamsters more than handling them, a dwarf species is a good choice. Dwarf hamsters are highly entertaining.

How Do I Choose the Right Species for Me?

> *If you are looking for a hamster that can be taken out of its cage and played with, I suggest the Syrian hamster—they are bigger and much more friendly than the smaller hamster species. For adults who are looking for a small pet that they can watch and interact with, but who may not have a lot of time for hands-on playing, I recommend a Robo hamster. They are the smallest of the hamsters and are so much fun to watch. The Dwarf hamster is also a great hamster but may not be the best fit for first-time owners, as you really need to know how to train them to handle one safely.*
>
> CINDY CRIBBS
> *Haven for Hamsters Rescue & Sanctuary*

It's tempting to choose your pet based simply on how it looks, but this is unwise.

You need to consider what you have to offer your pet, such as how much space you have available, how much money you have to spend on a habitat, and how much time you have to invest in caring for and bonding with your pet.

You should also consider the hamster's size, personality, and sleep cycle, as well as the age of the potential owner. Use the profile of each hamster below to help you decide which species of hamster is right for you.

Syrian Hamster

Size: 5–9 inches (average about 6 inches)

Friendliness: ◀▮▮▮▮▮▮▮▮▮▮▮▶

One or more can be in a habitat together: One only

Unique point: Syrian hamsters are available in a variety of colors and hair lengths.

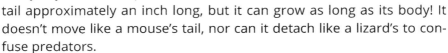

Chinese Hamster

Size: 3–5 inches (typically closer to 3 inches)

Friendliness: ◀▮▮▮▮▮▮▮▮▮▮▮▶

One or more can be in a habitat together: A pair of same-sex hamsters is possible if the introductions are handled correctly.

Unique point: This species has a tail approximately an inch long, but it can grow as long as its body! It doesn't move like a mouse's tail, nor can it detach like a lizard's to confuse predators.

Campbell's Dwarf Hamster

Size: 3 inches

Friendliness: ◀▮▮▮▮▮▮▮▮▮▮▮▶

One or more can live in a habitat together: More than one Campbell's can be in a habitat together if the enclosure is large enough to allow each hamster plenty of space. A pair of same-sex hamsters is typically the best arrangement.

Unique point: A bold, playful species that's fun to watch.

Winter White Dwarf Hamster

Size: 3 inches

Friendliness:

One or more can be in a habitat together if the enclosure is large enough to allow each hamster to have its own territory.

Unique point: These hamsters wake periodically in the day to play.

Roborovski Hamster

Size: 2 inches

Friendliness:

One or more can be in a habitat together: One only

Unique point: This is the smallest and fastest hamster species and also the friendliest of the dwarf hamsters.

CHAPTER 2

Setting Up your Hamster Habitat

I t's unlikely you'll be able to replicate a wild hamster's burrow, but hamsters today have been bred in captivity for generations, so they've never known that lifestyle. However, there are aspects of their natural environment you can bring into their habitat that are similar to their ancestors' natural surroundings.

The very first thing you'll need—which people often forget—is a secure, well-ventilated box in which to take your pet home from wherever you purchase it!

The Enclosure

> Hamsters need enclosures with lots of floor space to thrive and be happy. Cages sold for hamsters are typically too small and are not designed with a hamster's natural behavior in mind. Look for an enclosure with at least 600 square inches of unbroken floor space. The more space you can provide, the better! Clutter up your hamster enclosure with cardboard boxes, overturned mason jars to crawl into, 'hidey houses,' large tubes to crawl through, and other enrichment. An empty enclosure with not much to do will only bore and stress your hamster.
>
> JESSICA BRESLER
> *Poppy Bee Hamstery*

There's a wide range of habitats for you to choose from as housing for your hamster. These range from basic, one-level, rectangular wire cages to elaborate, multistory plastic palaces that include ramps or tubes for your pet to travel from one level to another. Many habitats are sold as part of a complete package of items you'll need for your hamsters, such as a wheel, water bottle, food dishes, and even bedding.

It's natural for you to think of this cage…

…as the usual housing for a hamster.

This is the type of enclosure you often see sold in pet shops all over the world. The most confusing thing you'll learn about owning a pet is that **not everything sold for pets is safe or healthy for them**. Sometimes the products are downright dangerous!

Cages and habitats need to be made of hard wire, stainless steel, glass, or plastic, as hamsters have strong teeth and can chew through enclosures made of softer materials.

Cages with wire bars may seem like an obvious option for a hamster habitat. The bars allow air to flow freely into and out of the cage, preventing dampness, condensation, and mold. Wire cages are easy to

HELPFUL TIP
Nocturnal Noises

Hamsters have incredibly poor eyesight and rely on their sense of smell, touch, and whiskers to navigate their habitat. Though these fluffy creatures are nocturnal (awake at night), they don't require light to see. It may be tempting to place your hamster's cage in a bedroom, but this setup may not be the best for you—or your hamster! Hamsters require a quiet place to sleep during the day and tend to be very active at night, which could impact your ability to sleep. Instead, consider keeping your hamster in a space that receives minimal daylight and will be quiet while your hamster sleeps.

clean and can be washed, disinfected, and dried.

The downside of cages with wire bars is that most hamsters chew on the bars for a variety of reasons. If the wire is painted, this means the hamsters can chew the paint off the bars, and the paint is often toxic. However, chew-proof coated wire is available on many hamster cages. If you discover your hamster is chewing on the bars of its cage, you can offer it something more tempting within the cage to persuade your hammy to chew that instead of the bars.

The gaps between the bars can also be dangerous for your hamster. The space between bars should be no more than a ½-inch. A young Roborovski hamster can squeeze through the bars of seemingly safe and standard-spaced barred cages. They can escape or become trapped between the bars. Make sure the doors and any other openings are secure, and there aren't gaps around them that are greater than a half inch. It's not fun to discover your pet has escaped through the bars, believe me!

Another thing to note before buying a habitat is how deep the base is and how easy it is to remove for cleaning. Even though a domestic hamster has never been out in the wild, it still has natural instincts, and one of those natural instincts is to burrow. It's advised that the habitat has a deep base—at least six inches. This is filled with bedding material to allow your hamster to fulfill its natural instinct to burrow, which will help keep your hamster's mind active and happy.

One of the key things to consider when you're deciding on a habitat for your pet is the size. This depends on several considerations—your hamster's needs, whether it will house more than one hamster, and where it will be placed in your house. Some cages sold in pet shops are barely 500 cubic inches. This isn't suitable for a hamster. It's cruel to contain a hamster that runs, on average, five miles a night in an enclosure this small. Regardless of whether you provide a wheel for your hamster, a habitat this small isn't safe or suitable. **Your hamster needs a minimum of 600 square inches of floor space—and 900 square inches if it's a Syrian hamster**. This can be over multiple levels. If the cage doesn't state the dimensions, it's possible to work this out by multiplying the length and width of the habitat by the number of levels the hamster has access to.

Be sure the height of each level is at least 18 inches—24 is best. This will allow for several inches of bedding as well as a wheel.

A tank cage—basically, a glass or plexiglass aquarium with a tight-fitting, clip-on, wire-mesh top—is a good option because it's basically escape-proof if the top is secure. Also, bedding can't escape the cage and make a mess. The downside of this type of enclosure is that it's not as easy to clean as a habitat that has a detachable bottom, so the entire tank must be cleaned. Glass tanks are heavy and will break if dropped. It's also necessary to make sure a glass or plexiglass habitat has plenty of ventilation. Nothing should be placed on top of the wire-mesh top that would inhibit airflow.

It's possible to create habitats in or with furniture to enable the hamster to have a large space while still fitting in aesthetically with the home. Furniture such as sideboards and cupboards can be used to create wonderful habitats. However, be aware that these might not be safe for hamsters if the furniture has been finished with paint or varnish or the wood it's built of has been treated with any type of chemical. The hamster may chew this wood, and that would be toxic to it. Even if your pet doesn't chew the wood, products such as varnish could make the hamster sick. Also, if the enclosure is made of wood, the habitat will be gnawed on and might eventually need to be replaced.

Crittertrail cages aren't recommended for hamsters because they're usually too small and don't have adequate floor space to allow the hamster to run around. In addition, the wheel included with these products is too small for larger hamster breeds such as Syrians. Also, the tubes that create the trails have multiple joints that can trap and breed bacteria from the usual soiling that happens as the hamster roams the trails. This overgrowth of bacteria can cause illness in the hamster.

The image below shows a cage with safe bars and adequate space for any size hamster.

Sleeping Area

Experts advise that you provide a minimum of two sleeping areas for your hamster to choose from. Often the sleeping huts that come with a hamster cage are small and plastic. Your hamster may use this, depending on its personality, but it's unlikely for two reasons:

1. A plastic hut is restrictive. Hamsters like to busy themselves by adding to or rearranging bedding in their sleeping area and sometimes storing food in it. A small hut means they can't do what comes naturally to them. The overall size of the plastic hut and the dimensions of its door are sometimes laughably small— barely large enough for a dwarf hamster to squeeze into, let alone the Syrian hamster it can supposedly house!

2. A plastic hut, while providing safety and being unlikely to be chewed up or gnawed upon (like a wooden or cardboard house would be), provides warmth but can also encourage condensation. This can cause food stored in it to grow mold.

While I don't have much good to say about plastic huts, that doesn't mean your hamster should be without a house altogether. Hamsters naturally want their sleeping area to feel safe and protected, so they require some sort of housing. This can be as fancy as a wooden lodge (that also doubles as a chew toy) or as simple as a cardboard box taken from your recycling, such as a tissue box. You'll likely have to replace this frequently because the hamster will likely chew it up. Personally, I use a coconut shell that's large enough for my hamster to fit into.

Bedding

Contrary to some people's beliefs, hamsters are extremely tidy creatures and like a clean house. Bedding should be warm and dry at all times. This will require you to remove dirty bedding when you find it and provide your hamster with fresh bedding as necessary. This can be fluffy cotton wool-type bedding or paper-based bedding. Tissues provide great entertainment for your hamster. It will spend hours ripping them to shreds and lining its bed.

Aspen shavings are the most appropriate type of bedding. Cedar and pine shavings are also available, but these shouldn't be used as regular bedding because they can cause respiratory problems for your hamster. There's a variety of other materials that are suitable bedding for hamsters, and commercial bedding is available at pet stores. Bedding that's at

Photo Courtesy of
Crystal Strickland

Hamster chewing on bars

least 10 inches deep is ideal for large hamsters, and the bedding should cover most, if not all, of the floor of the enclosure. This allows the hamster to burrow as it would do in the wild. Certain bedding materials such as aspen flakes, hemp shavings, and Care Fresh may not be rigid enough to keep the tunnels from collapsing. Adding layers of soft hay between bedding made of softer material may help maintain tunnel stability. Compacting the bedding also assists in maintaining tunnels.

Food and Water

Food bowls should be heavy enough that the hamster can't tip them over. Ideally, they should be made of porcelain or pottery. Most plastic bowls are too light, and hamsters will tip the food out to try and find the tastiest bits that might be at the bottom. This wastes food since hamsters often don't want to eat food that's mixed with their bedding. Also, plastic bowls are dangerous for them to chew on, even though they're inexpensive and easy to clean. Wooden bowls will be chewed and can be

Photo Courtesy of Finn Alford

dangerous, depending on whether the wood has been painted or treated. They'll need to be replaced, as well, if the hamster chews on them too much. Also, they cannot be disinfected properly, as the wood is porous and absorbs liquids—including potentially toxic disinfectants.

Pottery or porcelain bowls can be properly washed, disinfected, and refilled. They're also heavy and less likely to be tipped over. Make sure the bowl isn't so deep that your hamster can't easily have access to the food. If the bowl is too deep, smaller hamsters may not be able to get in and out easily, especially when they're young. Remember, just because something for a hamster is sold in a pet shop doesn't make it safe or appropriate. If you find the bowl you have is too deep, you can nestle it into the shavings, and that might make it easier for the hamster to retrieve food from it.

Water bottles can be glass or plastic. Make sure the size of the bottle is adequate and is properly fastened to the side of the habitat. You don't want it to fall off and be unaware that your hamster has no water. Water bottle covers can be a good idea, as water bottles that are exposed to sunlight can grow green algae that, while not poisonous or harmful, can be a nightmare to remove or prevent from growing back. You may find yourself needing to buy a new bottle.

Photo Courtesy of Molly Abrahams

When changing the water every few days, always check to make sure the nozzle is working.

I've seen a hamster become terribly ill because it couldn't access water as the ball in the mouthpiece became stuck and wasn't allowing water to pass. Hamsters, like all animals, need unrestricted access to water.

Food bowl

Water bottle

Cleaning the Habitat

> **"**
>
> *Cage cleaning is a must. Hamsters hoard everything, so you need to go in there on a regular basis to clean their cage. They may get very mad at you for ruining their home, but don't worry—it will give them something to do later when they go to 'rebuild!' We recommend completely emptying the cage and doing a deep cleaning about once a month.*
>
> CINDY CRIBBS
> *Haven for Hamsters Rescue & Sanctuary*
>
> **"**

Your hamster's habitat should be spot-cleaned daily. By this, I mean you should remove the shavings in the corner that the hamster uses for its toilet. Your pet will naturally select a corner far from its bed to use for toileting.

*Photo Courtesy of
Molly Abrahams*

Hamsters will push out of their sleeping area anything they don't want in there—old food, etc. Be sure to remove any vegetables or fruit that have been in the habitat for more than a day. If you do this, replace the food daily, and change the water every few days, you can go longer than you think before doing a full habitat cleaning.

When it's time to clean the whole habitat, put the hamster some-where safe. I put my Robo in the bathtub (empty, of course!) with the plug in and all possible methods of climbing out removed—such as a shower curtain or towels draped over the side of the tub. Hamsters are creative, and they're amazing acrobats! I line the base of the bath with newspaper and put cardboard toilet paper or paper towel tubes for tunnels and small open boxes for the hamster to explore while I'm cleaning the cage.

Photo Courtesy of Tina Keefe

Use water, dishwashing soap, and animal-safe disinfectants to clean the habitat. As long as the bedding and shavings are all-natural, you can put them into the compost bin. If they're made of something else, dispose of them in the trash. Wash all plastic or ceramic items, and dry them completely before arranging everything in the habitat. Save some of the bedding (the cleanest bits you can find) so the habitat smells familiar to your pet, which will make it more welcoming. Hamsters like the comfort of their own scent, and putting some old bedding in a newly cleaned habitat can reduce their stress.

CHAPTER 3

Hamster Nutrition and Diet

Even though they're rodents, hamsters are omnivores, not herbivores, as you might assume. A bag of nutritionally complete mixed dry feed specially created for hamsters is all your pet needs to have a basically healthy diet, but adding vegetables, fruit, and some type of protein will make your pet thrive. Some in the hamster community encourage supplements, but if your hamster's diet is truly balanced, they aren't necessary.

Feed your hamster its mixed dry feed once a day. You can supplement this with vegetables, fruit, and protein at any time during the day.

FUN FACT
Cheeky Rodents

Hamsters have the unique ability to stretch their cheeks with up to 20% of their body weight in food. This survival tactic allows wild hamsters to store extra food while gathering leaves, roots, or fruit away from their nest. Because these tiny creatures are easy prey for larger predators, they quickly collect their foraged items and carry them back to a safe place to eat. The name "hamster" actually comes from the German word "hamstern," which means "to forage."

How much you feed your hamster depends on its species, weight, and age. A Syrian hamster needs about two tablespoons of mix per day. Dwarf varieties only need about one tablespoon per day. If your hamster doesn't finish the food you give it within a day, or it's getting chubby, you're feeding it too much. If they eat all their food within a day, you may need to give them a little more.

A simple formula for a complete hamster diet is as follows:

The Mix

A Base Mix	Veg/herbs	Protein	Fruit
65%	15–20%	10–15%	5%
2 tbsp a day (Syrian or Chinese)/1 tbsp a day (dwarf species)	2 or 3 slices/cubes /sprigs	2 or 3 nuts/ mealworms/ 1/4 egg (half this amount for dwarf species)	a slice—less for dwarf species

Commercial hamster "kibble" foods are more likely to contain unnecessary fillers, sugars, and fats that could make your hamster gain weight. Some experts suggest feeding your hamster a pellet mix to prevent selective feeding; others say that if a mix is truly balanced, it shouldn't matter if hamsters pick and choose. By their very nature, hamsters are foragers and enjoy picking through their food.

The composition of the hamster mix varies depending on the species for which it's indicated. Syrians have different needs than dwarf hamsters

*Photo Courtesy of
Brooklyn Wegner*

or Roborovskis. Syrians originally came from areas in which a variety of cereals were grown, including wheat, oats, and rye. Roborovski hamsters, on the other hand, originated from a more arid land and enjoy smaller and more varied seeds in their mix.

Another fact surprising to many people is hamsters require animal protein. This only needs to be 10% to 15% of their diet, but it's necessary. This can be provided by feeding your pet a small amount of boiled egg or a few mealworms or nuts. Be aware that nuts have a high fat content, and this can cause your hamster to gain weight.

Vegetables, Herbs, and Fruits

In the wild, dwarf hamsters wouldn't naturally have fruit in their diet, whereas Syrian hamsters would. Stay away from prepackaged treats for your hamster, as they're full of fillers and sugar. Instead, supplement your hamster's daily food with fruit as a treat. Below is a table of possible vegetables and herbs to include in your hamster's daily diet, along with fruits to use as treats.

*Photo Courtesy of
Tracy Paul*

Safe Vegetables and Herbs

Arugula/rocket leaves	Ginger
Artichoke	Green beans
Asparagus	Kale
Beetroot	Mushrooms
Basil	Mint
Bell peppers	Parsnips
Bok choi	Peas
Broccoli	Potatoes (cooked)
Brussels sprouts	Pumpkin
Cabbage	Radicchio
Carrots	Romaine lettuce
Cauliflower	Soybeans
Celery	Parsley
Corn	Spinach
Cucumbers	Squash
Dill	Sage
Edamame	Sweet potato (cooked)
Endive	Swiss chard
Fennel	Zucchini

*Don't forget about grass and edible flowers too!

Safe Fruits

Kiwi	Kumquats
Apples (no seeds)	Lychees
Apricots	Mangos
Bananas	Nectarines
Blackberries	Papayas
Blueberries	Passion fruit
Cantaloupe	Peaches (no pits)
Cherries (no pits)	Pears
Cranberries	Pineapple
Currants	Plums (no pits)
Dates	Pomegranate
Elderberries	Raspberries
Figs	Starfruit
Gooseberries	Strawberries
Grapes (no seeds)	Tomatoes (ripe)
Guava	Watermelon
Honeydew melon	

You'll notice that most of the seeds and pits of fruit shouldn't be fed to your pet, and you might wonder why. After all, hamsters like seeds, don't they? The problem is that some fruit seeds and pits contain cyanide, which is a poison. Now, a human would need to eat a lot of the seeds and pits to feel unwell, but your hamster is tiny in comparison to you, and there's a good chance the level of cyanide contained in just a few seeds would be enough to kill your pet. The pits and seeds also contain nothing nutritionally beneficial and are a choking hazard.

Photo Courtesy of Dana Balatsos

There are a number of foods that you should NEVER feed your hamster. I've listed them in the chart below. These foods are either bad for hamster health (potentially resulting in obesity or diabetes) or they're toxic/poisonous (the bolded items) and could result in the death of your pet. It's easy to make a mistake, so be aware!

Hamster Food No-Nos!

Red meats	Ham/cold cuts
Fatty junk foods	**Citrus fruit**
Chocolate	**Almonds**
Rhubarb or rhubarb leaves	**Raw beans**
Onions	Any sugary foods, e.g., cookies/cake
Garlic	Anything salty
Uncooked Potatoes	**Fruit pits/seeds**

The Importance of Clean, Fresh Water

As mentioned previously, your hamster must always have access to clean, fresh water. The water should be changed at least every few days, and the ball in the nozzle should be checked twice a day to be sure it's working and dispensing water.

CHAPTER 4

Hamster Health

Common Hamster Illnesses

> " Finding a vet who actually knows how to treat hamsters is an absolute must. Not every vet knows how to care for hamsters, and just because a receptionist says they'll see hamsters doesn't mean that they really know how to treat them. Ask the pet store which vet they use or go online and ask around in hamster groups. It is very important to have a well-qualified vet for your hamster because oftentimes, once you know your hamster is sick, you'll only have a very short window to get it treatment.
>
> CINDY CRIBBS
> *Haven for Hamsters Rescue & Sanctuary*
> "

The focus of this chapter is to alert you to signs and symptoms that indicate your hamster may not be well. If your hamster shows any signs of illness, contact your veterinarian immediately. Don't attempt to treat your hamster without seeking veterinary advice. Keep your hamster as comfortable as possible until your veterinarian is able to see it.

"Wet Tail"

Wet tail is one of the most common illnesses that afflict Syrian hamsters. Without treatment, a hamster can die in a matter of days. It's called "wet tail" because the most noticeable symptom is wetness around the tail and hind end caused by the diarrhea that characterizes this disease. It will look like your hamster sat in a puddle.

CAUSES   Wet tail is caused by bacterial overgrowth in the gut. Stress is the biggest cause of the overproduction of bacteria that results in the gut environment becoming out of balance.

SYMPTOMS   Your hamster may exhibit loss of appetite; dehydration; dampness on the butt, tail, and tummy; decreased activity; and weight loss. Your hamster could have one of these symptoms or a combination of several.

TREATMENT   The hamster should be seen by a veterinarian immediately to receive fluids and/or antibiotics. Once home, wash the soiled tail and tummy in saline solution regularly for as long as the hamster has diarrhea to prevent the bacteria from being redigested when your pet tries to clean itself. Leave the hamster alone as much as possible and in as stress-free an environment as you can create.

Pneumonia

Pneumonia is a bacterial or sometimes viral infection of the lungs that causes inflammation and breathing difficulties. Although pneumonia isn't frequently seen in hamsters, it's second only to wet tail as the most common potentially fatal disease in these animals.

CAUSES

The bacteria that cause pneumonia are normally present in the respiratory or digestive system in small numbers. These bacteria can multiply and lead to illness when the hamster becomes stressed by sudden changes in its environment—especially temperature fluctuations. Stress makes it more difficult for the hamster's body to fight the infection.

SYMPTOMS

Your hamster may have discharge from the nose or eyes, difficulty breathing, loss of appetite, and lethargy.

TREATMENT

If you suspect your hamster may have pneumonia, see your veterinarian immediately. Your veterinarian can diagnose pneumonia by examining your pet or performing laboratory tests. Often, treatment isn't effective, but antibiotics can help in mild cases. Fluids may be administered via injection.

Once your hamster is home, you can assist its recovery by keeping its habitat warm, clean, and dry and making sure nothing stresses your pet. If it has cage mates, isolate your hamster at the first sign of illness and immediately clean the habitat where the other hamsters are living.

Colds

Hamster colds are very similar to human colds. It's important that you don't handle your furball when you're sick because you can transfer your cold to your hamster! The amount of virus that causes a cold in a hamster isn't strong enough to make you ill, but a cold in a hamster can cause death.

CAUSES A hamster can catch a cold by being held by someone who's unwell or being near other unwell animals (such as in a pet shop).

SYMPTOMS Your hamster may act lethargic. Its ears may be flat against its head. Its nose might be swollen, or there may be discharge from the nostrils. There might be a wet look around the eyes. If the cold is particularly bad or the illness has progressed, the hamster can look thin, its coat will be disheveled and dull, and you may even hear a sneeze or a cough.

TREATMENT Disinfect the cage immediately—the water bottle, the bowls, everything. Also, change the type of bedding you're using. Sometimes what appears to be a cold may be an allergic reaction to the bedding.

It's better to be safe than sorry, so take all precautions if you suspect your hamster may have a cold. Move the cage to a warmer location to avoid drafts, as sick hamsters can lose body heat quickly. Make sure there's lots of extra bedding available. Provide your hamster with high-quality food to boost its immunity. Warm milk or baby food adds more calories to your hamster's diet for energy. Some experts suggest using a few drops of cod liver oil on the food to aid recovery but seek veterinary advice before doing this. If your hamster doesn't respond in a day or two, consult your veterinarian.

Constipation

Constipation can be a serious health issue for your hamster as it can indicate a life-threatening intestinal blockage. You might notice fewer or no droppings in the corner that your hamster usually uses for toileting. If you notice no droppings for more than a couple days, call your veterinarian.

CAUSES Constipation can be caused by the hamster drinking insufficient water if its diet is primarily dry pellets. The dry pellets swell inside your hamster's intestines, and if there isn't sufficient water to break them down, this can cause a blockage. We'll talk about dehydration shortly.

TREATMENT Check the hamster's water bottle to be sure it has water in it and that the ball in the nozzle is working. You might consider putting several bottles in your hamster's habitat on different levels to provide extra opportunities for the hamster to drink. This also helps avoid the problem of an empty or nonfunctioning bottle. Make sure you change the water at least every few days. This is a must.

Provide your hamster with fibrous vegetables such as carrots, broccoli, and kale. Maybe add a few drops of olive oil to its food, as this is a natural laxative. As mentioned previously, if there hasn't been improvement in a couple of days, consult your veterinarian, who may prescribe your hamster a laxative.

Diabetes

Diabetes (diabetes mellitus) is uncommon in hamsters, with the exception of the Chinese hamster, especially if the hamster is a product of inbreeding. Dwarf breeds of hamster are more prone to diabetes in general. Diabetes is actually several endocrine diseases, all of which derive from the pancreas not producing enough insulin (referred to as Type 1 diabetes) or the cells of the body not responding properly to the insulin produced (insulin-resistant diabetes, referred to as Type 2). This leads to an increase in blood sugar (glucose) in the bloodstream, which has negative effects on several body organs and systems. Type 2

diabetes is much more common than Type 1 and can often be treated with changes in diet and exercise. If untreated, diabetes can lead to many other health complications.

SYMPTOMS
There are a number of symptoms that indicate your hamster may have diabetes:

Increased appetite
Insufficient insulin causes a loss of energy in the body. As a result, the appetite increases as a way to try to compensate for this loss of energy. However, overeating doesn't solve the insulin issue.

Excessive thirst/drinking
As glucose levels increase in your hamster's bloodstream, its kidneys become overwhelmed. The kidneys excrete

these high levels of glucose into the urine. This process requires more than the usual amount of water from the body, which means your hamster will be thirsty all the time.

Excessive urination

Because your hamster is drinking more water, it will be urinating much more frequently and in larger volumes than normal.

Hyperactivity and/or lack or energy

Because diabetes affects the metabolism and other aspects of your hamster's body, energy levels fluctuate. This means your hamster may sometimes be hyperactive and, at other times, will be lethargic.

Loss of weight

Because glucose isn't available as a source of energy, your hamster's body will use fat and muscle tissue as an energy source. If the diabetes isn't treated, this will result in weight loss and muscle wastage. Even though your pet may be consuming more food, the energy from that food isn't able to be used by its body.

Urine smells sweet

Excess glucose in the urine causes the urine to have a sweetish smell, which is a common indicator that the hamster has diabetes.

If you see any of these symptoms—especially excessive drinking and urinating—there are some steps you can take at home to determine if your hamster might have diabetes. There's a product called Keto-Diastix that can be purchased over the counter at pharmacies. This tests the urine to determine the presence of glucose or ketones.

To do the test, place your hamster in an empty plastic box and wait until it urinates. This shouldn't take long if it has diabetes because of its increased water intake. Dip the test strip into the urine and compare the color of the urine on the strip with the chart on the Keto-Diastix packaging. If there's glucose or ketones in the urine, this suggests your pet has diabetes, and it's time to visit your veterinarian. Even if the test doesn't indicate diabetes, if your hamster has the symptoms mentioned above, it's good to consult with your veterinarian.

TREATMENT

As mentioned previously, diabetes in hamsters can be treated with diet, weight management, and, if needed, medication. Diabetic hamsters must always have access to plenty of fresh water, and their habitats need to be cleaned more often than for a hamster that doesn't have diabetes because the excess glucose in its urine can easily grow bacteria and make your hamster more susceptible to bladder infections.

Diabetic hamsters need a more restricted diet than healthy hamsters, but the diet still needs to be well-balanced. Review what you've been feeding your hamster. Any foods that are high in sugar—not just added sugar but naturally occurring sugars such as fructose found in fruit or corn syrup—should be avoided. There are commercial hamster mixes that have no added sugars, are low in natural sugars, and provide a nutritionally balanced diet. Hazel Hamster Food is one such product. Avoid giving your hamster store-bought hamster treats, as almost all of them are high in sugar. The less sugar you feed your hamster, the less stressed its body will be, which means it will be healthier and happier.

Simple carbohydrates (carbs) such as sugar, most fruit, white rice, pasta, and bread should also be limited because they're difficult for the body of a diabetic hamster to break down and convert to glucose. Most processed foods—crackers, pasta, etc.—are high in simple carbs.

Complex carbs are an excellent substitute, and there are many foods that contain complex carbs that your hamster will love—broccoli, kale, low-sugar fruit like berries, cooked brown rice, cooked beans, and oatmeal.

Feed your diabetic hamster a high-protein and high-fiber diet. Diabetic hamsters should have a diet that's 10% to 15% protein and 50% fiber. Supplement their regular hamster mix with sources of protein such as plain tofu, cooked chicken or turkey, or scrambled egg. Only small amounts of these foods should be given to your hamster each day.

Good sources of fiber include alfalfa, timothy hay, and vegetables such as broccoli, cucumber, cauliflower, and spinach.

Even though it drinks a lot of water, a hamster with diabetes is prone to dehydration due to excessive urination. I'll talk about how to diagnose and treat dehydration in your hamster shortly.

Getting plenty of exercise is critical if your hamster has diabetes. Your pet should have a large enough habitat that it has lots of room to run around. A wheel is essential for a diabetic hamster, and there's evidence that hours of running in a wheel each night can prevent or delay the onset of diabetes in some hamsters.

Lastly, your diabetic hamster may benefit from medication. However, the dosage of this medication must be spot on, or serious health complications or even death may result. Glipizide and fenugreek are common oral medications prescribed for diabetic hamsters, but these must be dosed by a vet. Glipizide tablets are crushed into a powder, mixed with water, and then fed to the hamster. Fenugreek is available in tablets or powder that can be brewed into a tea and given to the hamster. However, it can be difficult to control the dosage.

Insulin may also be indicated as a treatment for your diabetic hamster. Your veterinarian will show you how to give your pet injections, and you'll do this usually twice a day. Because hamsters are such small animals, care is needed to determine the correct dosage of insulin, and this may need to be adjusted over time. If the hamster receives insulin, its glucose levels must be checked weekly to see how it's responding to the medication.

Dehydration

Dehydration means the normal amount of water in the hamster's body and tissues is too low. Because hamsters are so small, they can become dehydrated quickly. Water is lost naturally through urination, but too much water can be lost if the hamster has diarrhea or diabetes. Dehydration affects all functions in the body and can also upset the balance of electrolytes, which can be life-threatening.

CAUSES

Diarrhea is the primary symptom of wet tail, and this is a leading cause of dehydration in hamsters. A hamster with wet tail can become dehydrated in a matter of hours after the first appearance of symptoms. This is why it's necessary to seek treatment immediately if you notice your hamster has diarrhea.

Another possible reason for dehydration is that the hamster isn't drinking water. This is usually because of a dysfunction in the water bottle in which water isn't being dispensed properly when the hamster tries to drink. This is why it's so important to check to be sure the water bottle is functioning properly.

If the water bottle is working, you need to next determine how much water your pet is drinking. To determine this, mark the level of the water in its bottle and check it in 12 hours. Most hamsters drink 10 ml of water per 100 grams of body weight per day—or about a third of an ounce for a hamster weighing 3.5 ounces. Dwarf breeds drink very little water, so it might be difficult to determine if water is being consumed unless the bottle is relatively small.

Excessive drooling is often a sign of a tooth or mouth problem, and this can contribute to dehydration.

SYMPTOMS

The hamster appears listless and weak. Dehydration severely taxes your hamster's body, so it won't be active or interested in its usual activities, including eating. It will likely huddle in a corner or spend most of its time in bed sleeping. The hamster may have a dry, warm nose. The hamster may appear to have lost weight due to the loss of water volume in its body.

- To test for dehydration, gently pull the skin between the hamster's shoulder blades away from its body and then release it. See how quickly the skin returns to its normal position. If the skin immediately relaxes, that indicates the hamster is well hydrated. If the skin remains in a pinched shape, the hamster is dehydrated.

TREATMENT

Because dehydration can be so deadly for hamsters, if you suspect your pet is dehydrated, take it to your veterinarian immediately. If the hamster is indeed dehydrated, the vet will administer fluids under the hamster's skin (subcutaneously) since hamsters are too small to receive fluids by intravenous (IV) infusion.

If your hamster has an underlying condition that's causing dehydration, such as wet tail, the vet will administer or send you home with medication to treat that illness. In rare cases, your pet may need to be hospitalized to determine the cause of the dehydration.

If your hamster is showing signs of dehydration, and you're unable to take your pet to a vet immediately, here are a few things you can do at home until it can be seen by a professional.

- Substitute unflavored Pedialyte or other electrolyte solution for its drinking water. Pedialyte can be found in most grocery stores. Place the hamster's water or Pedialyte in a shallow dish so it's easy to access. If the hamster is severely dehydrated, it may be too weak to get to the nozzle of the water bottle.
- See if your hamster will eat slices of a juicy fruit or vegetable such as cucumber, peeled apple, or lettuce.

Rehydrate your pet manually using an eye dropper or small syringe (no needle). Hold the hamster firmly but gently, and place a drop of water on his lips every half hour. Don't put more than one drop at a time (or it may go up your pet's nose and be aspirated into its lungs), and no more than a drop every half hour.

Of course, much better than treating dehydration is preventing it in the first place. First, check your pet's water bottle at least once a day to make sure it's working properly. The metal ball at the end of the nozzle should move freely and allow a drop of water to escape when depressed into the nozzle. If the water bottle is working fine, and your hamster has access to it, lack of water isn't the problem.

NOTE: If you've just gotten your hamster, it may never have seen a water bottle before. It may have been fed water from a dish, so it doesn't know how to operate the nozzle. If this is the case, you can gently squeeze the sides of the bottle to make a drop of water appear as a bead on the end of the nozzle. This should be enough to attract the hamster to the bottle, and as it licks the bead of water, that will activate the metal ball to release another drop of water.

If you don't see or hear your hamster drinking water from the bottle within a few hours of arriving in its new home, put water in a shallow dish in the corner of its habitat. Make sure the dish isn't easily tipped over since a wet hamster is more likely to become a sick hamster.

The environment of the room where you keep the hamster is essential to its overall health, including its risk for dehydration. The ideal temperature for your pet is 68°F to 75°F. Be sure the enclosure isn't in direct sunlight, near a heat source, in a drafty area, or in a cold corner.

Offer your hamster a mix of dry, commercial hamster food and fresh fruit, vegetables, and other hamster-safe foods. However, feeding your pet too many high-water-content fruits and vegetables can cause digestive problems in your hamster that lead to diarrhea. For this reason, cucumbers, lettuce, apples, watermelon, and other juicy produce should be fed to your hamster sparingly.

If your hamster is stressed, it may refuse to drink. Hamsters can become stressed by new situations, too much handling, an abusive cage mate, overly curious pets and children, and loud or startling noises. So, be sure your hamster's habitat is located in a quiet room, and it has plenty of alone time in between play periods.

Hairballs or Intestinal Blockage

During the process of bathing, hamsters may sometimes swallow fur, so it's natural for them to have hair in their stomach and digestive tract. The hamster's body is adept at removing any hair buildup, and the excess hair is incorporated into the animal's droppings. Hairballs or blockages caused by clumps of fur are rare in hamsters, but long-haired Syrians are susceptible to these issues.

CAUSES

Hairballs and hair-related blockages may occur in hamsters that are unwell and shedding or excessively cleaning themselves (which they may do if they have mites or are stressed). A low-fiber diet can create issues, as can dental disease or mouth pain.

Hairballs occur because hamsters are unable to vomit, so they can't eject any foreign objects—which is what a hairball is—from their stomach. Because they can't vomit, the hairballs have only one way to go—into their digestive tract! Often a hairball will move through their digestive system without causing a problem, but there's always a chance it can completely obstruct the intestine. This is dangerous for small omnivores like hamsters, and they can't survive long with a blocked intestine. Plus, this is an exceedingly painful condition that will cause your hamster to suffer before it eventually dies.

SYMPTOMS

Unfortunately, it's not easy to know if your pet has an intestinal blockage. In the wild, there are many animals that prey on hamsters, so hamsters are naturally good at concealing illness or injury, as sick or lame animals are likely to be eaten first. Hamsters will often pretend that everything is fine to encourage predators to attack something else.

If you suspect an intestinal blockage, look for any of the following signs. Any of these could indicate other problems, but they're common if there's an obstruction in the digestive tract.

Decreased appetite
If your hamster isn't interested in its usual food, try offering it a treat. If it refuses its favorite snack, try again in a few hours. If it isn't eating and still won't accept a snack, it's best to visit the vet.
The only time a hamster may not eat even its favorite snack is when it's out of its habitat. Hamsters won't stop to eat if they feel scared or uncomfortable because if they stop moving to eat, they're more vulnerable to predators.

Decreased fluid intake
It's necessary for hamsters to drink throughout the day, so make sure the water in the bottle is visibly less each day. If

it isn't, first check the ball bearing in the mouthpiece of the tube with your finger to see that it's working by pushing the ball in or rolling it. A single water drop should come out. A hamster can't survive long without drinking and needs a veterinarian's attention immediately if it's not hydrating.

Issues with Droppings
Hamsters have a rapid digestive process and produce droppings at regular intervals throughout the day and night. If you notice the toilet corner is bare, keep an eye out.

If you notice the droppings are linked together with hair (like a necklace), this could indicate a hair blockage.

If you notice any watery droppings as opposed to dry, rice-shaped droppings, your hamster needs to see a vet immediately. This could indicate a blockage or an infection and needs immediate intention.

Unfamiliar noises
You'll become accustomed to your pet's everyday noises. Some hamsters are very vocal, greeting you with all sorts of squeaks; others never make a sound. Either is normal. It just depends on your hamster's personality. However, if you hear your hamster making noises you haven't heard before, look out for other symptoms that may indicate it's ill. Talk to or visit your vet to make sure your hamster isn't making this noise out of pain or discomfort.

A change in character
If your friendly, cuddly hamster suddenly bites you during playtime, this can be shocking. The first thing you should do is to put your pet back into its habitat and leave it alone for a while. If the behavior continues, see if you can figure out a reason for its change in temperament. Has something happened recently, like a change in diet or a new habitat? If everything is normal with the hamster's environment and routine, there might be something wrong,

and that might include an intestinal blockage. Animals in pain will lash out.

TREATMENT   Is your hamster sleepier than normal? Does it not greet you at the door of its habitat as usual? We all have good and bad days, even hamsters! But if the change in behavior continues, it might be time to visit the vet. The hamster could be dehydrated, there might be a blockage, or the animal might be in pain.

Lumps and Bumps

If you discover a lump or bump on your hamster, it could be a number of things—a cyst, a fat deposit due to obesity or age, or cancer.

CAUSES   You could be overfeeding your hamster with sugary foods and treats. If the overall size of your hamster hasn't changed, there's a chance that nothing you've done has caused the lump. It's important to have a veterinarian check it out, however.

TREATMENT   You can take your hamster to the vet, and they'll probably do a biopsy of the lump or bump to determine what it is. If it's a cyst, the fluid within it can be aspirated with a needle. If it's a fat deposit, there's no reason for concern. If the hamster is overweight, the bump may reduce in size by feeding your pet a reduced-calorie diet. It might be a benign (not cancerous) lump that's neither a cyst nor a fat deposit. If the lump is cancerous, you and your veterinarian will have to discuss whether surgery is an option that will provide a cure or prolong your pet's life or if the cancer has already spread, and therefore, surgery isn't indicated. There are also the considerations of whether you want to put your pet through the trauma of surgery, as well as the cost of the procedure.

Something Suspicious

> " Be on the lookout for diarrhea—this is a health care emergen-
> cy and requires vet care. If the hamster is constantly scratching
> or itching itself and losing fur, a vet should also be consulted, as
> this may mean the hamster is suffering from mites. Always be on
> the lookout for weight, activity, or behavioral changes in general,
> as those are some of the only indicators of problems we'll see as
> hamster owners.
>
> MIKAILA HUDYM
> *Cloverline Hamstery* "

HEALTH ALERT
Beware of Salmonella

Though uncommon, hamsters can carry salmonella, an intestinal bacterium that can cause serious illness in humans. As a result, the CDC recommends washing hands thoroughly with soap and water after handling hamsters. It also suggests refraining from kissing hamsters, eating or drinking near hamsters, or allowing hamsters near where food is prepared. Identifying a hamster with salmonella is problematic because it will usually appear healthy. However, if a hamster develops salmonellosis (a salmonella infection), symptoms can include fever, lethargy, vomiting, and other concerning indications.

Because hamsters are so small, it can be extremely difficult to diagnose and treat them. That being said, I recommend that you trust your instincts. If your hamster isn't following its natural routine or it just seems "off" in some way, consult your veterinarian. You can't play the "wait-and-see" game with an animal as small as a hamster. An illness can become life-threatening in a very short time.

Sometimes your veterinarian won't be able to diagnose with certainty what's wrong with your pet. The minuscule size of a hamster relative to a dog or a cat means that a lot of vet equipment isn't useful for

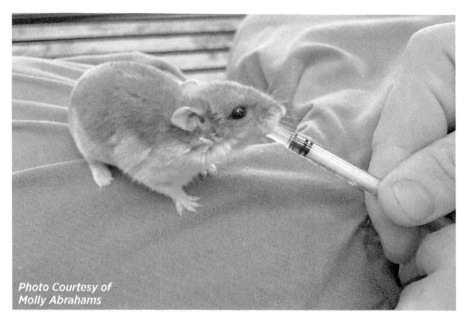

Photo Courtesy of
Molly Abrahams

such small bodies. The vet may simply tell you they don't know what's wrong and send you home to see what happens. If your hamster isn't enjoying life anymore, and isn't eating, drinking, or playing, you may have to make the difficult decision to euthanize your beloved pet. You don't want your hamster to be in pain, even though it's heartbreaking to say goodbye to it.

Euthanasia is a medical procedure performed by a vet to bring about an easy, peaceful death rather than your pet dying slowly from its illness, which can cause it significant suffering.

Euthanasia involves an injection or a gas or sometimes both. An injection of a painkiller makes your pet sleepy, and then it's overdosed with a drug that stops its heart. With small animals, gas is used more often than an injection. The animal is put into a sealed container, and an anesthetic mixed with oxygen is pumped into the container via a tube. As the animal breathes in this odorless mixture, it falls asleep, and the overdose of anesthetic stops its heart. If an injection is used, you should be able to hold your pet as it passes away. The vet will confirm your pet's death by listening for the cessation of the heartbeat with a stethoscope.

Paying for Medical Care

> *Hamster care isn't free, and it can be costly, but it is less expensive (relatively speaking) than vet costs for a cat or dog. Remember: by taking on a hamster as your pet, you are also taking on the responsibility of providing it with as happy and pain-free of a life as possible. Some of my hamsters have had very little medical care, while others have needed things like X-rays or minor surgeries. During the course of my hamster's lives, I might spend between $200 to $800 on medical expenses. If you need to start saving now, I highly suggest it! Vet care expenses can vary depending on where you live, but there is nothing more painful than watching a hamster whom you love suffer.*
>
> RACHEL ARNSDORF
> *Rachel Got Hamsters*

Photo Courtesy of Crystal Strickland

There's no other way to say this—veterinary care is expensive. For this reason, I recommend that every pet owner purchase medical insurance for their pet, whether they have a horse or a hamster. Owners sometimes decide not to get medical insurance coverage for a small pet, but this can be unwise. Small animals can become quite ill quickly, and their tiny bodies can be overcome in hours rather than days or weeks. As soon as you notice something is wrong, it's imperative that your pet see a vet within 24 hours. A work-up (imaging, lab tests), surgery to remove a lump, and follow-up medications and consults could set you back thousands of dollars.

HELPFUL TIP
Hibernating Hamsters

Hamsters thrive in temperatures between 65°F and 75°F, the average temperature of most temperature-controlled homes. If a hamster's habitat dips below this ideal threshold for an extended time (more than 24 hours), the hamster may enter torpor, a state similar to hibernation. True hibernation occurs if a wild hamster's winter environment is frigid or food is scarce, but pet hamsters should not hibernate. You can prevent torpor by keeping your hamster's cage between 65°F and 75°F, providing adequate bedding, and checking on your hamster frequently.

You don't want to be in the awful position of having to euthanize your hamster for a condition that could be remedied with medication or surgery because you don't have the funds to pay for its medical care. A small monthly premium will not only save you from spending thousands for treatment, but it could also save your hamster's life.

Familiarize yourself with your local veterinarians to find out who has experience treating hamsters, and choose your preferred vet before you need to take your hamster to them. You don't want to be in an emergency situation and have to call around trying to find someone who's qualified and available to see your pet. This could be a fatal oversight.

The best way to choose your vet is to talk to friends who own hamsters or look at online reviews by the veterinarians' clients, especially any that mention the care they received for their rodent. Sometimes you'll only have your instincts to rely on when you suspect your hamster is feeling poorly, so you need a vet who takes your role as a caring pet owner and your suspicions seriously.

If possible, try to find a veterinarian who specializes in small animals, not just dogs and cats. "Small animals" includes birds and aquatic pets, so try to find a doctor with a track record in treating hamsters, gerbils, mice, rats, and rabbits. A vet who specializes in aquatic animals, for example, may have a more difficult time diagnosing what's going on with your hamster than someone who studies and treats rodents specifically.

CHAPTER 5

Hamster Behavior, Enrichment, and Bonding with your Pet

t can be disappointing if your hamster seems fearful when you get it home—especially when you're so excited to have this new friend and want to play with it.

Try to be empathetic toward your new pet. Your hamster may have been living with its mother and siblings, and now it's suddenly in a big new habitat all by itself. Even if it was living on its own before, this new home doesn't look the same or smell the same. The hamster might even have had an additional stop in between being with its mother and arriving at your house—residing for a while at a pet store. Its interactions with humans may have been minimal, and it may not have been handled a lot, and this will cause the hamster to not be immediately comfortable with someone it just met—you.

HELPFUL TIP
Puzzle Toys

When you think of puzzle toys for pets, hamsters probably don't come first to mind. But these small rodents are natural foragers who enjoy toys that challenge them to find food. Hamster puzzle toys are available from various retailers and are usually made from wood (an essential element for healthy hamster teeth!). Though small, hamsters are surprisingly intelligent and will amaze you with their ability to master new and challenging toys. Unfortunately, understimulated hamsters may become aggressive, lethargic, and destructive.

Hamsters love routine, and its life so far may have had a lot of stress. When you pick up your hamster from the breeder or the pet store, ask them to put a little of the animal's bedding into the box you'll be taking it home in. If they're a person who cares for their animals' welfare, they might even suggest this themselves.

Once you get home, put the old bedding with the new bedding, as this will ease some of the animal's stress. This helps your hamster identify that its new habitat is safe/home. Your new pet may move the location of its bed, but it will often use the same bedding materials.

It takes time for your hamster to adapt. A hamster craves calm, quiet, and solitude when it first moves into its new home, and it's vitally important that you allow your hamster to settle in without disturbing it.

Allow your hamster at least 24 to 48 hours before you touch it. Watch it for stressed behavior. These signs will be similar to the behavior of a fearful or anxious human. Your pet might move around the edges of its cage when it should be sleeping. It may seem restless, dig in its bedding constantly, not eat, or sleep all the time.

Photo Courtesy of
Diana Sydnor

If you see any of these behaviors, don't pick up your hamster. Stress can overwhelm your hamster's small heart and kill it. Take this opportunity to give your pet some treats through the bars and talk to it. Get it used to your voice. Keep doing this until you see your hamster has established a routine—eating, drinking, and sleeping during the day, and running on its wheel at night. Like humans, hamsters use exercise as a stress reliever, so check regularly that the wheel is in good working order and spinning freely.

During this settling-in period, only remove the hamster from its habitat if it isn't out and about by the evening to make sure it's okay. Check for a runny nose, crusty eyes, or wheezing. This could signal respiratory problems and may mean there's something in the habitat that isn't healthy for your hamster. Disheveled fur can mean the hamster contracted mites while at the pet store. If you have a concern about how your hamster looks or is behaving, contact your veterinarian to do a check-up.

When it appears that your hamster has calmed down and is enjoying its new home, you can begin to remove your hamster from its habitat several times a day, but only when it's awake. You're just beginning your relationship, and you don't want to start this friendship by wrecking your pet's sense of happiness and security by grabbing it out of its habitat. Encourage the hamster to the door by placing something yummy by the exit. It might take your pet a little time to catch on, but soon the hamster will connect your visit with the treat, and it will be running to greet you when you call its name.

Understanding Your Hamster's Behavior

> "
> *Hamsters are crepuscular prey animals, which means that they are naturally active at dawn, dusk, and sporadically throughout the night. It is natural for them to wait for the lights to go out before emerging from their burrow. If you find that your hamster is being a hermit, wake it up by luring or digging it out of the burrow. Some folks feel guilty for disturbing them, but overall, hamsters benefit from human interactions. You can also recalibrate your hamster's schedule by turning the lights on for 12 hours a day—especially in the winters. They will usually come out once the lights have been off for an hour or two.*
>
> STEPHANIE WINGER RODRIGUEZ
> *Pearl Hamletry Hamsters*
> "

Unfortunately, your hamster is unable to talk to humans, and you, I'm pretty sure, can't speak hamster. For this reason, you need to pay attention to your hamster's behavior to try and guess what might be going on. Here are some common hamster behaviors and what they mean:

Hissing: This sounds like an angry bee, and it means your hamster is agitated. If you're holding the hamster, put it back into its habitat immediately, as it's likely you're moments away from a bite!

Squeaking: Hamsters squeak when they feel scared or anxious. You might hear your hamster squeaking during the time it's settling into its new house. The squeaking sounds a little like hiccups. Personally, I think it sounds sad, like squeak-crying. Sit by its habitat and talk to your hamster if it's evidencing this behavior so you're building a relationship of companionship.

Grooming: Your hamster needs to groom, and if it does this in your presence, that means it feels comfortable. Take it as a compliment. However, if your pet is grooming excessively and you notice places where there's no fur, this means your hamster might have anxiety or mites. If you suspect the latter, take your pet to the vet ASAP.

Chewing: Hamsters must chew on hard materials because their teeth never stop growing. Chewing is how they keep them worn down and of the correct length. If the teeth become too long, this can be life-threatening, and they need to be seen by a veterinarian. This creates an unnecessary and hefty bill that you can avoid by providing toys and hard foods for your pet to chew on.

Often hamsters chew on the bars of their habitat. Your pet may do this to try to get your attention and let you know it's bored. If this is the case, find something for it to play with that will draw its attention away from this annoying bad habit.

Sleeping during the day: Hamsters are nocturnal, just like owls and bats. Remember, hamsters are prey for many animals, so they come out at night, hoping that, under the cover of darkness, they're less likely to be attacked. Also, some breeds originated in the desert, where it's too hot or even dangerous to be out during the day. If your hamster is eating, drinking, and active at night, sleeping all day is perfectly healthy behavior.

There are many different items that work well as toys for your hamster. A new texture, a new smell, or something new to chew on can help keep your hamster happy. And you don't have to spend lots of money on toys. Anything can be a toy! Just follow a few rules when choosing something to entertain your pet:

Photo Courtesy of
Molly Abrahams

- Toys comprised of sawdust and glue can be fatal to your hamster. Check the components of all toys.
- Exercise wheels made of metal wire or bars or that are too small can create back issues and may break a tiny leg.
- Tunnels: As mentioned previously, if a tunnel is too small, your pet can get caught in the tube and injure itself. Also, remember that your hamster will stuff its cheeks with food or bedding, and if it tries to travel down a too-narrow tube with this material in its cheeks, it can suffocate or choke!
- Cuttlefish bones are suitable for birds but not for rodents. They're not a good toy.
- Salt licks are sold as a nutritional supplement for rodents, but they're unnecessary if your hamster has a balanced diet. Salt cubes were created for rodents used in scientific settings (e.g., animal testing facilities.) If you feed your hamster properly, you don't need to buy these.
- Pumice stones and lava ledges: Anything made of pumice or "lava stone" isn't a good abrasive material to wear down your hamster's teeth. Although some experts agree that these stones can be a good way to file down the teeth, there have been reports of small animals choking if they manage to bite off a piece of the stone. Other people have found that many hamsters have no interest in them, and they're a waste of money.

- Cardboard food boxes: Boxes are fine as toys for your pet as long as they're free of paint and don't contain anything that could be toxic to a hamster. Make sure all staples, tape, and glue residue have been removed.
- Dig boxes: Besides digging tunnels in their bedding, hamsters love to dig in general, so you can provide your hamster with a "dig box" containing coconut fiber, cork granules, or sphagnum moss.
- Sand: Hamsters—especially those whose ancestors lived in the desert—love to roll and play in sand. They also use it to groom and dig in. Make sure the sand you provide is animal-safe and approved for hamsters. This isn't the same as the sand you find on the beach! Sand suited for other animals can be too fine, and when your hamster is frolicking in it, the sand can be breathed in and cause respiratory problems. For example, sand for Chinchillas is too dusty for hamsters. Play sand or reptile sand with no dyes or calcium is a good choice. A glass baking dish makes a great sandbox.
- Hamster balls: The value of these toys is up for debate. They used to be a staple of any hamster's setup. I remember using them with my first hamsters. The idea behind the hamster ball is that the animal is able to roam around the house within a rolling enclosure, so it has a sense of running about but in a way that it can't get lost or hurt. However, in my opinion, the benefit of using the hamster ball is for the human, not the hamster.

FUN FACT
Forwards and Backwards

Hamsters can run backward nearly as quickly as they can run forward. This unique ability is likely a survival adaptation to help them escape their underground burrows rapidly when faced with a predator. So keep a watchful eye on your hamster's tunnels to see this talent in action.

In recent publications, experts have deemed that a hamster ball is stressful for the animal. As with exercise wheels that are too small, the balls bend hamster spines in an unnatural way, which can be painful and cause damage. The plastic also inhibits the hamster's senses. Hamsters have poor eyesight in comparison to their other senses, and by depriving them of those senses, the hamster is rolling around blind. The gaps for air in the ball are small, but so are the feet of most hamsters! They can catch their feet in these holes, and broken toenails, toes, feet, or even legs can result. Ventilation within the hamster ball can be an issue if the air holes become plugged with debris or droppings that prevent air from getting through.

Before you purchase a hamster ball, consider the potential negatives I've just described. As I mentioned, I put my hamster in the bathtub while I clean its habitat because I know she can't get out as long as I've checked to make sure there's nothing she can climb up on to escape. I can put toys in there for her to play with. I also close the bathroom door in the remote chance she finds some way to get out. She'd be confined to the one room, so she couldn't get lost somewhere in the house, and she'd be safe from my cat or from any other dangers.

Photo Courtesy of Brooklyn Wegner

Under your supervision, you can provide all sorts of adventures for your hamster. I put my hamster in a pile of clothes for her to explore or in a fold-up sweater, so she can tunnel out of the arm holes. It's fun to watch. Keep a close watch on your hamster if it's on your bed, as hamsters will jump—or fall—from the height of your bed or sofa to the floor and can hurt themselves. They can squeeze into the smallest of places and be easily lost. Your hamster may object by squeaking if you pick it up when it's having great fun on the bed, but you don't want it to come to harm.

Enrichment

Enrichment is a necessary part of the physical and mental health of your hamster. Hamsters need space for burrowing so they can create tunnels. They also need other forms of enrichment. That isn't to say that all hamsters will enjoy all the enrichment options you offer. It comes down to their preferences and their personalities.

Wheels are a necessity for almost any hamster. Remember, these critters run up to five miles a night! Twenty-eight centimeters (about 15 inches) is the appropriate diameter of a wheel for a Syrian hamster. To decide if it's the right size, have a look at your hamster while it's running. Its back should be virtually straight, not bowed. This unnatural curvature can damage your hamster's spine.

For smaller hamsters, you may wish to consider a running disk. These are virtually silent, which wheels may claim to be but rarely are. However, discs take up more floor space as they're arranged horizontally rather than vertically.

A wheel is the minimum your hamster will require for enrichment as well as exercise. Other enrichment could involve any of the following:

Hay, dried flowers and grasses, sand baths, wooden steps, hanging mobiles, empty jars, balls, food cages, nutrient blocks, toilet paper tubes, hanging baskets, ladders, mazes, problem-solving games— the list goes on!

Anything with a variety of smells and textures to keep your hamster's mind stimulated and busy is a good choice. Vary these enrichment materials, and remember to make sure they're as natural and unscented as possible to keep your hammy safe!

Building a Bond with Your Hamster

> "
> It takes time and patience to create a good bond with your hamster. Consistency is key—hamsters love their routines, and it is the owner's responsibility to set up regular handling sessions in the evening so the hamster will learn to expect and enjoy interaction. A hamster that is awake, alert, and indicating interest in coming out of the enclosure is a happy hamster who is ready to play. Giving treats also helps your hamster learn to trust you!
>
> JESSICA BRESLER
> *Poppy Bee Hamstery*
> "

Remember that building a relationship with your hamster is a marathon, not a sprint! Many hamster owners feel frustrated by how long it can take to build a bond with their pet. I read an article by a hamster expert who stated it took eight months before their pet hamster, a Roborovski named Steven, allowed them to pet it. At the opposite end of the spectrum is my hamster, Num-Num, who became completely infatuated with

HELPFUL TIP
Can Hamsters
Cohabitate?

Whether hamsters prefer to live alone or in pairs depends on the species. While some hamsters are content to share their space with a sibling or companion, others can become fiercely territorial. For example, Syrian hamsters strongly prefer to live alone and may fight other hamsters in the same enclosure. On the other hand, dwarf hamsters will usually tolerate company. To avoid mishaps with hamster pairings, provide multiple feeding areas and ensure the cage is large enough for two. In addition, do not house hamsters of opposite genders together unless you plan to breed this pair.

me the day we met and has had a friendly, sociable nature since day one.

A hamster's personality and attitude toward people can be greatly influenced by their experience with humans from an early age. Pet shops sometimes breed hamster pups on a large scale with a fast turnover, which means there's a chance the hamster you purchase hasn't been handled by any human. It might associate human hands with being removed from safety and security—like when it was taken from its mother and moved to a cage in a pet shop or the box you brought to take it home.

There might be trauma and negative associations with humans that you'll need to heal before a relationship can form with your new pet. Hamsters bought from reputable breeders may have been handled and have memories of humans giving them treats and love, so they may warm up to you a lot quicker.

There are many ways to form positive bonds with your hamster. Playtime is a great opportunity. Set up a playpen with lots of toys and things for your hamster to explore. Scatter and hide treats so the hamster makes the connection between the fun of playtime and time spent with you. Sit in the playpen and allow the hamster to crawl over you without grabbing after it. This will show your pet there's no pressure to form a relationship with you. Some hamsters will progress to sitting on your lap or shoulder willingly without luring them with treats. You can watch TV while your hamster rests in your lap. But other hamsters, no matter the length of time you've spent together, will remain nervous and suspicious. This has nothing to do with you and may just be the creature's character.

Patience and consistency are the keys to creating a lasting relationship. Try to interact with your pet at the same time each day. Soon, you'll see your hamster waiting for you by the door of its habitat, ready for playtime.

NOTE: Hamsters are often purchased for children who are too young to look after them. Make sure an adult is dedicated to supporting the child in caring for the animal, as children often lose interest in the hamster, leaving the animal unloved and unstimulated—and perhaps without food and water—in its habitat.

CHAPTER 6

Grooming and Hygiene

> " Hamsters, like all rodents, have teeth that constantly grow. Hamsters self-maintain their teeth length through grinding and 'bruxing.' Contrary to popular belief, they do not require chewing items to help maintain their teeth, but providing chews does still offer them wonderful enrichment! Cardboard scraps and hard-shelled nuts are two good options for safe chewing.
>
> JESSICA BRESLER
> *Poppy Bee Hamstery* "

Grooming your hamster could involve bathing, trimming nails, and brushing. This is also a great opportunity for you to check the hygiene and overall health of your hamster's ears, eyes, and teeth.

Brushing

Brushing your hamster should only be necessary if it is a long-haired Syrian hamster. To groom this animal, buy a thin-toothed comb that's designed for animal fur. Human hair is a lot thicker than fine hamster fur, so human combs won't work. Brush your pet *gently* once a day to help remove loose fur. This will help prevent your hamster from developing stomach problems caused by ingesting its fur.

Other than this, the hamster shouldn't need your assistance with maintaining its coat. If its fur looks scruffy in any way, that could indicate a problem or illness. A visit to the vet is probably in order.

You can identify whether your hamster isn't grooming its coat in a few ways:

Long Haired Syrian Hamster

- The hamster's fur seems to be clumped together. This is called matting, and while it may seem like an aesthetic issue, it can become a serious condition that can threaten your hamster's life. So, if you notice a knot in the fur, do your best to remove it as soon as possible with a brush, a comb, or even your fingers. If matting becomes a regular problem, you can buy something called a finger brush that helps to separate the knotted fur. A toothbrush can work well for this purpose, too. Be gentle as you loosen the knot or mat, and don't pull your pet's fur out, as that can be painful!

If you can't get rid of the mat with simple tools, or the clump has debris in it that's keeping the fur stuck together, you may need to trim that area. I'd personally use a pair of cuticle scissors. Try to do this with your hamster standing with all four feet on the surface rather than flipping it on its back. This will stress your hamster, and it will thrash about, which could endanger it, especially if you have scissors in your hand. However, if it's necessary for your pet to be on its back so you to reach the tangle, you need a second pair of hands to hold your hamster firmly while you do the trimming.

If a mat isn't removed, more fur can become entangled in it until it's a hard knot. This can cause irritation or wounds on the hamster's skin or even cut off blood flow to an area. In a worst-case scenario, your hamster could lose a limb!

If you're unable to remove a knot or mat, seek guidance from a veterinarian.

- You may notice the hamster's fur is soiled in places, and debris may be caught in it. If the fur is soiled or clumped near the hamster's bottom, this could indicate illness. Clean the area with lukewarm water and dry it completely (otherwise, your hamster could catch a cold), and see if the problem returns. If it does, it means the issue is persistent and requires a vet visit.

Hamsters take great pride in being clean, so there's certainly an issue if you find that your hamster isn't keeping up with its personal hygiene.

Bathing

> Hamsters are very clean animals when given the necessary supplies. Every hamster loves to bathe its coat by rolling around in terrarium sand. The same way humans use shampoo to maintain the oils in their hair, hamsters roll in the sand. If sifted and baked, children's play sand is also safe for hamsters, and any glass or acrylic container can be used as a sand bath tray. Because hamsters are prey animals, rolling on their backs in the sand puts them in a very exposed position. But adding a 'hide' to the sand bath for them to bathe underneath will help them feel safer!
>
> TABITHA HULTQUIST
> *Happy Hamstery*

Hamsters typically bathe themselves once a day. You'll see your pet sitting on its hind legs and using its front paws to clean itself. They look very cute when they do this! Hamsters lick their paws and then wipe them over their faces, just like cats do. Hamsters bathe their entire bodies in this way.

Is It Necessary for You to Bathe Your Pet Hamster?

A normal, healthy hamster doesn't usually need bathing. Plus, if a hamster is bathed too often, it can destroy the natural balance of oils in the fur and skin.

There are a few circumstances where bathing may be necessary:

- **Overweight hamster.** Hamsters developed dense, thick fur to provide protection and warmth in the wild. The hamster's body itself is slender and flexible, enabling it to fit into all sorts of tight spaces. If your hamster is fed too many treats or an improper diet, it can become overweight. Besides not being healthy for your hamster, your pet may find it difficult to bend and bathe itself. It's important that your hamster be fed a healthier diet with fewer calories to shed excess weight. Stop giving it treats and provide it with lots of low-sugar vegetables. Your hamster will have its favorites, but I'd encourage you to feed it celery, cucumber, and lettuce. These are all low-sugar and low-calorie vegetables. Vegetables high in nutrients and fiber, such as kale, spinach, and bok choy, are also great to mix into their food.

Until your hamster loses weight, it may be necessary for you to bathe your pet in the places it can't reach.

- **A disabled hamster**. It's unlikely you'll have a hamster that's disabled, but if your hamster becomes injured and unable to clean itself, a vet may suggest you temporarily bathe your pet. If it's permanently disabled, you'll have to do this routinely.

- **A hamster with wet tail.** A hamster's back end may become soiled and wet if the animal is suffering from diarrhea. It isn't good for the hamster to clean itself in this case, as it will re-ingest the bacteria that's making it ill. Use saline solution to clean the hamster's back end.

How to Bathe a Hamster

- Use a small container, such as a Tupperware box.
- Fill the container with lukewarm water up to the height of the hamster's shoulders. The hamster should be able to stand in the water on all fours with no danger of drowning. Don't add water to the container with the hamster in it!
- Make sure the container has high sides to prevent the hamster from escaping the bath.
- Gently place the hamster into the water, encouraging it to feel comfortable by enclosing it in your hands. Once the hamster is calm, use a teaspoon or, even better, a pipette to wet its back. Your hamster's undersides and legs will become wet by them standing in the water. If your pet is moving too much for you to apply water to its back safely, support the hamster with one hand while gently washing it with the other. Be careful to avoid its face.
- Use only small-animal-friendly shampoo from a pet shop. To work the shampoo into the hamster's fur, start at its back. Squirt a pea-sized amount of shampoo onto a soft brush such as a toothbrush or a paintbrush, and gently rub the shampoo into the hamster's fur all over. Make sure you don't get shampoo into the hamster's eyes. Rinse them quickly

FUN FACT
Long in the Tooth

Like all rodents, hamsters' incisors never stop growing. Our small furry friends keep their teeth worn down to a manageable size by gnawing. The name "rodent" comes from the Latin word "rodere," which means "to gnaw." If a hamster's incisors grow too long, they can interfere with eating or cause painful cuts inside the mouth. Providing your hamster with adequate chew toys, including pesticide and chemical-free wood toys and cardboard, is crucial. Some hamsters prefer to eat dog biscuits, but check with your veterinarian before offering these treats.

with lots of water if you do! Rinse the shampoo out of your pet's fur thoroughly with water from the pipette or teaspoon. A damp face cloth might help to get rid of the final suds. Hold your hamster in one hand and wipe gently with the cloth over its body.

- Once washed, move your hamster onto a fabric or paper towel to dry naturally, though I imagine your pet will be moving pretty fast and be desperate to escape. Make sure you dry your hamster in a heated room without drafts. A hamster can succumb to cold easily and die from hypothermia. However, hairdryers are too loud, too hot, and too powerful, so don't use any devices to dry your hamster. Never put your hamster back into its habitat when it's wet or cold.

Nail Trimming

Truthfully, I can't imagine a situation that would require you to trim your hamster's nails. A hamster's nails, like our own and those of many other animals, grow continuously. It's necessary to provide different textures of flooring in the habitat or at playtime so these surfaces can naturally file the hamster's nails down.

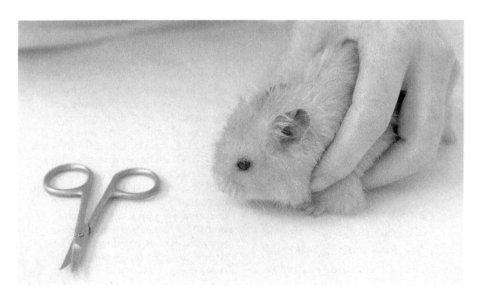

The only situation in which a hamster's nails are excessively long is if you've rescued the animal from a neglectful situation. If this is the case, it's probably best for a vet to trim its nails.

If you're an expert at working with hamsters, feel you need to clip its nails, and there's no veterinarian nearby to do this, you can try trimming the nails when the hamster is calm and happy. Use nail clippers, not scissors, to trim the nails. It's best to take a little off the nail at a time, as you can always go back and trim some more. However, you really need to know what you're doing because if you cut too much, you may cut off the end of the hamster's toe. Besides causing your pet tremendous pain, there will be a lot of blood—not to mention creating an infection risk. My advice is—don't trim your hamster's nails. It's not necessary, and it's risky.

CHAPTER 7

Hamster Safety and First Aid

It might surprise you to know all the things in your home that might hurt your hamster. Always supervise your hamster, as these little creatures are crafty escape artists. Make sure that wherever you play with your hamster, it's enclosed and safe.

As far as safe food is concerned, please refer to the earlier chapter for the list of foods that are toxic for your hamster.

Common Household Dangers

Electrical cords are a tempting toy for your hamster. Their texture makes them appealing as something to chew on, but your hamster could receive an electrical shock powerful enough to stop its heart.

Ovens, the back of the fridge, and behind radiators all offer lovely and warm hiding locations if your hamster escapes from its habitat. The problem is, if you haven't found the hamster before you need to use one of these appliances, you might burn or harm your hamster.

Any water sources that aren't fresh water from a bowl or bottle are unsuitable for your hamster.

A hamster's small body can be easily overtaken by germs, bacteria, or poisons. You might think to yourself, "I don't have poison lying around," but some household cleaners are unsuitable for cleaning your hamster's habitat, especially if you don't rinse the habitat correctly, leaving residue.

Things that are poisonous for your hamster can come from all sorts of places:

Photo Courtesy of
Dana Balatsos

- It's common for people to give their pets leftovers, but moldy food could kill your hamster.
- Certain paints and materials used in household decorations might be poisonous for your hamster or prove to be potential choking hazards. The safety of human toys and household items hasn't been tested with hamsters in mind.
- Most household plants are toxic to a hamster. Below is a noncomprehensive list of common plants and flowers that might be around your

house. If any portion of these plants finds its way into your hamster's habitat, it could be fatal. Believe me, it happens!

Toxic plants include autumn crocus, azalea/rhododendron, coto-neaster, Cordyline/dracaena, daffodil, dumbcane, horse chestnut, oak, peace lilies, potato plants, and yew.

The easiest way to avoid your hamster coming into contact with any of these potentially harmful household items is to set up a play space that's enclosed. It's easy to accidentally leave something on your bed, like a bit of chocolate, and later, when you're playing with your pet, the hamster finds it and eats it before you can stop it. Death by poison can be slow and painful, so if your pet does consume something harmful, seek medical attention straight away. Don't wait until the hamster starts to display symptoms. By then, it could be too late.

Hamster First Aid

While I always suggest seeking medical treatment from a veterinarian if your hamster becomes injured or appears ill, sometimes you might find yourself in a situation that requires you to act immediately, or veterinary care isn't easy to access. Maybe something happens to your hamster in the middle of the night, and there's no emergency veterinary care available in your area. This means you'd have to wait hours until the vet's office opens for your hamster to be seen. Maybe your hamster has cut itself, and you need to stop the bleeding before going to the vet because your hamster is at great risk of dying without first aid.

Photo Courtesy of Molly Abrahams

Prior to an emergency, make sure you have a ventilated pet carrier to transport your hamster. You'll be more likely to be seen immediately by a veterinarian who already has your hamster as a patient. You need care that you can access swiftly. Some vets won't see pets that aren't their patients. Also, in an emergency, you don't want to be calling around trying to find somewhere that has an immediate opening. This will increase your stress as well as the risk to your hamster.

HISTORICAL FACT
Domestic Hamster Origins

Syrian hamsters are believed to have been the first species of hamster domesticated as pets. These creatures were introduced in America in 1938 and were wildly popular only a few years later. Some believe all domesticated Syrian hamsters are descended from one wild hamster captured with her litter by medical researchers in 1930 in Aleppo, Syria.

Below are some suggestions for a hamster-themed first aid kit.

- **1 milliliter (ml) syringes** (without needles) are useful for administering water or liquid oral medication. The doses of medication for a hamster are extremely small, and syringes used to administer human medications are usually at least 5 ml in size. You may have to look around to find ones that are only 1 ml.

Small syringes can be useful for giving your hamster water, liquid food, or rehydration solutions to a dehydrated hamster.

- **Cotton balls and Q-Tips** can be used to apply small amounts of cream or liquid to cuts or bites. Young hamsters usually get along fine with one another—until they don't. Also, if you're planning on breeding your hamster(s), the hamsters you're trying to pair might fight when introduced. I remember one of my dwarf hamsters and his brother always got along really well together. Then, one day, for no apparent reason, my hamster, Roubal, was attacked by his brother. Roubal ended up with a nasty bite on his nose. Q-Tips were perfect for cleaning the wound and applying antiseptic solution. My current hamster, Num-Num, used to fight with her sisters, and she now has a rip in her ear that required first aid when she first got it. In situations like this, a Q-Tip allows you to apply medicine while maintaining a safe distance from a potentially angry and frightened animal.

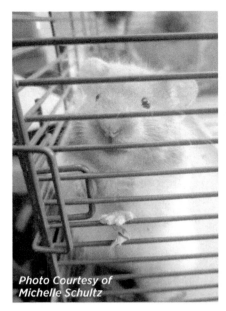

- **Animal-safe heating or cooling pads** can be used in winter and summer underneath your pet's habitat to warm or cool your hamster's living space as needed. Some products are can be placed inside the hamster's habitat. However, you need to be very careful that heating devices aren't so hot that they burn your pet or cooling

Photo Courtesy of Michelle Schultz

devices don't make it too cold if it's near them. Of course, hamsters are likely to nibble on these devices, so be sure the product is chew-proof and the contents of cooling packs aren't poisonous for pets. Many contents of many cooling packs designed for humans would be poisonous for a hamster.

Your hamster's habitat should be inside the house, out of direct sunlight, away from drafts, and in a room that's heated during cold weather. The habitat shouldn't need assistance from a heating or cooling pad to maintain correct temperature. In extremely warm weather, it might be necessary to place a cooling pad under part of the floor of the habitat. Don't have the pad under the entire floor, but leave an area that isn't cool for the animal to go to if it wants to. In any case, have a place where the hamster can cool down and regulate its temperature.

Here's a list of essential items to have on hand to make sure your hamster stays safe or that you can use in a situation where first aid is required:

- **A food scale** is a great way to measure your hamster's weight. Keeping track of its weight is critical, especially if it's unwell. Weight loss is an indicator of something untoward going on with your hamster's health.

- **Face cloths** can be useful to wrap your hamster in to stop it from wiggling while you give it medication. A face cloth is great because hand-feeding your hamster and giving it medication can get messy!

- **Saline solution** is excellent for cleaning scratches, bites, or burns. In a pinch, cold boiled water (boiled and left to cool) with a sprinkling of sea salt dissolved in it also works.

- **Baby food** can be fed to a pet that's recovering from an illness or surgery. It's high in sugar and easy to process. Make sure the food doesn't have too much protein (i.e., nonvegetarian baby food) or other ingredients that wouldn't be good for your hamster.

- Teas that may be helpful in an emergency:
  - **Black tea** contains tannins that help coagulate blood from a bleeding wound. For this purpose, place five tea bags in a cup of hot water and leave them to sit for two or three minutes. Saturate a cloth or a cotton pad in the tea, and then hold it against the wound until the bleeding stops.
  - **Thyme tea** is made by steeping a handful of fresh thyme in hot water. When cool, this can be used on a cloth to disinfect a wound in an emergency.

CHAPTER 8

Hamster Reproduction and Breeding

Female hamsters and male hamsters are easy to identify by their genitals.

Female hamsters have internal and external reproductive organs. Internally, they have ovaries, a uterus, and a vagina. Externally, they have a vulva. Although hamsters only have two mammary glands (the organs that produce milk), they can have anywhere from six to 16 nipples!

Male hamsters have no nipples, unlike male humans. They have a penis, which spends most of its time hidden in the fur, and the testicles of adult male hamsters are large in proportion to the size of their body. This makes it easy to identify your hamster's gender.

Hamster Reproduction

Hamsters, like most rodents, are super reproducers! The gestation period for a Roborovski hamster is 23–30 days, and that

FUN FACT

Baby hamsters are called pups!

of a Chinese hamster is 21–23 days. Dwarf species, like Campbell's and Winter White, have a gestation period of 18–21 days, and Syrian hamsters reproduce the quickest of all hamsters, with a gestation period of only 16–18 days. Syrian hamsters can become pregnant during every estrous cycle, which happens every four days! That means a Syrian hamster can produce up to 18 litters a year, with each litter containing an average of six to eight pups, although there have been instances of 12 to 20 pups in one litter. That means one female Syrian hamster can produce over 100 pups a year!

Female hamsters can start to reproduce at just four to six weeks old, and mating can happen in a matter of seconds, so don't mix genders after your hamsters are three weeks old. In addition, the hamster species that enjoy company in their habitat, such as Chinese hamsters, prefer to be housed with animals of their own gender. If the opposite gender is introduced, say, a female into a habitat with males, this creates competition among and aggression in the male hamsters. Females are usually even less hospitable to the intrusion of a male, so there's a chance of injury if a male hamster is introduced into an all-female habitat.

A caring hamster owner doesn't want his or her hamster(s) to be reproducing willy-nilly. An owner who makes a mistake in deciphering the gender of their hamster(s) can become quickly overrun. Your veterinarian should be able to gender your baby hamsters. I speak from experience. I've never misidentified the gender of my hamsters, but I've done so with three pet mice. All three were supposed to be females, but I discovered the hard way that "Miss" Maple was actually "Mister Maple." I was shocked to find 10 little mice pups in the habitat when I was cleaning it one day! Like hamsters, mice can get pregnant immediately after giving birth. Long story short, I made one mistake about gender, and I had 35 mice popcorning all over the cage. They were cute, but it was a bit of a nightmare.

Spaying and Neutering

Spaying is the common term used to refer to the removal of reproductive organs from a female animal. Neutering is the term used to refer
to the removal of the reproductive organs from male animals, although
castration is another word that's also used.

Hamsters aren't generally spayed or neutered because it's risky to
use anesthetic on such a small animal. Typically, anesthesia isn't used on
such a tiny animal unless it's a life-or-death situation. It's so easy to give
the animal too much anesthetic, and that stops their breathing and their
heart. The only safe alternative to spaying and neutering is to separate
male and female hamsters before they reach reproductive age.

Breeding Your Hamster

As mentioned, hamsters can become sexually mature at four weeks
of age, so it's important to have hamster pups separated by gender if
you don't want any surprise litters. If you decide to breed your female

HELPFUL TIP
Where Are
Hamsters Illegal?

Before breeding your hamsters, you must check with your local government to ensure that your hamster operation is legal. Certain states and countries outlaw hamsters or specific hamster breeds due to the risk escaped hamsters pose to local ecosystems. For example, pet hamsters have been banned in Hawaii, New Zealand, and Australia because of ecological concerns.

hamster, doing so when she's between 10 weeks and 15 months is a safe timeframe.

As the female goes through her pregnancy, she'll need more high-quality food and more water—and maybe a few more treats. Pregnant and nursing hamsters require more energy and, therefore, need extra protein, as well as vegetables and fruits rich in vitamins A and E. Food quality is important, as it will assure strong, healthy pups and a mother that's in good physical shape. Since your hamster won't want to interact with you for a while after giving birth, providing a balanced diet with plenty of calcium, vitamins, and protein to build her strength and make sure she has plenty of milk is a great way to show your love and support. Pregnant females need extra nesting materials as well to prepare for and welcome the litter of pups.

Pregnant hamsters can be quite aggressive, so give your pet her space. Its belly won't become obvious until a few days before giving birth. You'll know when your hamster is close to giving birth because she'll be restless and may pace in circles around her habitat. When you see this behavior, try to do a final cleaning of the habitat before the birthing, as it will be a while before you can clean it again. Just before birthing, your hamster will make a large nest, and she won't emerge from it until her pups are delivered. Some owners set up a small camera within the nest a week or so before the birth to be able to see if the hamster has had her babies without disturbing her.

Once your hamster has given birth, you need to leave her alone for seven days, even if you fear for the babies. The reality is you won't be able to help the babies if they're in trouble. If you disturb the mother and babies, you're likely to stress your hamster, and stress can lead her to

abandon her babies or worse—eat them! So, the best thing you can do is leave her to it. This will give the pups the best chance to grow up healthy.

After seven days, you can tidy the habitat, remove debris from the nest, and maybe catch a quick look at your new family members! At 14 days, you can start to pick up and cuddle the mama hamster. She may be feeling tired and stressed and not want to be held. In this case, give her a few more days. Alternatively, she may be desperate for a break from the babies and want some human contact. Just follow her lead.

This is also a great time to start handling the pups and getting them used to humans. Early handling is one of the benefits of getting your hamster from a breeder as opposed to a pet store. Hamsters raised by breeders will be familiar with household noises, children, and being held.

At three weeks, the pups should have stopped nursing and be eating a normal hamster diet. You may need to crumble food and/or add water to make the food more manageable for the pups' tiny mouths.

New homes should be arranged for your pups before they're four weeks old. You'll notice your mama hamster will want time apart from her pups and may spend time out of their reach if it's possible. Give her breaks in her playpen, but not for too long, as the mother and babies might get anxious if separated for too long.

CHAPTER 9

Senior Hamsters

U nfortunately, the lives of hamsters are very short in comparison to other pets. In the wild, the average lifespan of a hamster is two to three years, but domesticated hamsters typically live for three to four years.

A wild hamster has a shorter life due to threats that it doesn't have to contend with as a pet that you're taking excellent care of. Wild hamsters have to cope with extreme weather conditions. They also have to constantly search for food and not fall victim to predators. Deforestation

Photo Courtesy of
Francesca Perrotta

and changes in climate can lead to loss of habitat, food shortages, and other environmental challenges.

There have been cases where hamsters in captivity have lived longer than four and a half years, but these instances are rare. Poor diet, too-small cages, limited exercise, and boredom reduce pet hamsters' lifespans, as do interbreeding and overbreeding. Some Dwarf breeds may only live a year. Hamsters stop being able to breed at about 14 months, and by 18 months, any hamster, regardless of species, is considered a senior.

When your hamster reaches seniorhood at about a year and a half in age, this might mean you need to make some adjustments to its habitat, routine, and lifestyle to accommodate any old-age difficulties.

Caring for an Elderly Hamster

> *Elderly hamsters may sleep more and prefer to stay hidden in their nests. Respect their need for space and quiet, but make sure their food and water are easily accessible. Offer them their favorite foods and treats more often, and make sure to keep their room at a favorable temperature.*
>
> JESSICA BRESLER
> *Poppy Bee Hamstery*

Just like elderly humans, certain activities can become a struggle for hamsters as they age because their bodies just don't work like they used to. A two-year-old hamster is equivalent to an 80-year-old human. Hamsters are already fragile creatures, but when they get old, they can become even more vulnerable to illness and injury. So, gentle care is a priority.

Sight, hearing, and other senses might become less sharp, meaning your hamster may need help recognizing where things are in its habitat.

FUN FACT
World's Oldest Hamster

According to Guinness World Records, the oldest recorded pet hamster lived to 4.5 years old and was owned by a woman in the UK. Unfortunately, the hamster's name is not registered, but he was owned by Karen Smeaton. Typically, hamsters only live 18 to 36 months in captivity, and Syrian hamsters have the best chance at longevity.

It's not uncommon for hamsters to get arthritic. You might also notice parts of its habitat aren't being used anymore, and treats may go untouched on upper levels of the habitat. You may notice your pet no longer sleeps in the bed on the top level, or it may be making its nest near the food bowl. Due to hearing loss, your hamster may not come to you when you call like it used to, or for other reasons, your pet no longer comes to the door to meet you or for its evening treat as it once did.

These are all symptoms of aging and mean you need to change things in your pet's habitat, such as providing less steep ramps and no vertical climbs for your hamster as it travels around the habitat. If the current habitat is too challenging for your hamster because of age-related disabilities, it's time to move it into a one-level enclosure. This might confuse your hamster at first, but it will be better in the long run. Your aging hamster may be relying more on its sense of smell, so place some old bedding in the new habitat when you transfer your hamster to help it feel at home and secure.

When you relocate your hamster into a new habitat, put the bowl of food and the water bottle relatively close to the bed area. Gradually move the bowl and water farther away each day for a few days so your hamster is aware of their location. It might also be necessary to lower the water bottle or provide water in a bowl if the hamster is struggling to reach the nozzle of the water bottle due to stiffness or back problems.

Infections and diseases occur more often in older animals, just like in humans, so cleanliness is important to prevent your hamster from getting ill. Daily spot cleaning is a must. Your pet might not be as house-proud as it once was as it becomes less able to keep things tidy, so you may have to help out a bit more by removing stored food before it molds, changing soiled bedding—which is likely to happen more frequently as the hamster ages—and changing the water and food every day.

You might notice your hamster may sleep more and in more random places. Try not to worry; this is just part of aging. Place bedding material around the habitat so the hamster always has a place to be warm and comfortable.

Change in Diet

> *When a hamster is more than a year and a half old, I generally advise adopters to stop giving snacks that are high in protein. Pups do well with some egg or chicken during their growth phase, but a senior hamster does not need the extra protein, and it can actually create a lot of work for aging kidneys (especially for males).*
>
> MIKAILA HUDYM
> *Cloverline Hamstery*

Checking your hamster's front teeth as it ages is a great way to keep track of what sort of diet you should be feeding your pet. If the teeth are short enough that the hamster can close its mouth, it's chewing on its toys regularly, and it eats all its food without leaving any pieces behind, your hamster should be fine to continue eating its current diet.

Front teeth that are broken or overgrown can interfere with your hamster's ability to eat. If your hamster is experiencing any difficulty eating, you should take your pet to your veterinarian so overgrown teeth can be filed down or removed as necessary.

If your hamster starts to experience dental issues, it might be time to alter its diet.

Creating a More Appropriate Diet for a Senior Hamster

- If you feed your pet pellets, add a little water to them so the pellets break down and create a mush. Weetabix is a great source of fiber and can be soaked in water as your hamster ages.

Photo Courtesy of Karen McQueen

- You can give your hamster vegetarian baby food if chewing has become too difficult. Baby food contains necessary nutrients and is of a consistency that's easy to eat. Sugars in the food provide your hamster with energy. However, if your pet is overweight, choose baby food containing green leafy vegetables such as spinach, kale, and cabbage, and stay away from sweet vegetables like corn, sweet potato, and carrots.
- Hamsters need protein but can struggle to process insects and meat. Boiled or scrambled eggs are a great alternative.
- Remove hard shells from nuts and seeds to help prevent cracked teeth.
- Steam vegetable sticks.

It's normal for your hamster to lose weight as it gets older. Its face will look thinner, and the spine will become more prominent. These signs could be mistaken as symptoms of illness, but if your pet is eating and drinking regularly, doing some exercise, sleeping during the day, and toileting normally, it's probably having a healthy old age. Try not to take your pet to the vet unless you feel it's an emergency situation, as such trips are stressful for your hamster and could interrupt its eating and willingness to move about its habitat. You only need to take a senior hamster to be checked if it seems to be in pain or is unable to eat, drink, or toilet. Otherwise, the best thing you can do for your aging pet is just adapt to its new routine and allow for change.

Don't be surprised if your senior hamster eats and drinks less. As it becomes less active, it needs less energy and, therefore, less food. The immune system of your hamster becomes weaker as a natural part of aging, so in addition to making sure its environment is clean, it might be necessary to add dietary supplements.

Supplements for Senior Hamsters

- **Vitamin C** promotes your pet's health. Without it, a hamster may contract a painful disease called scurvy.

Symptoms of scurvy include fur loss, lethargy, squealing when touched, weight loss, and the pet becoming hunched and wobbly when walking. Broccoli and citrus fruit are great sources of vitamin C.

- **Vitamin D** is known as the sunshine vitamin because mammals absorb it through their skin by being in the sun. However, it's unwise to leave your hamster's habitat in direct sunlight, as your pet can become dehydrated and overheated. Cod liver oil is high in vitamin D. Coating your hamster's food with a teaspoon of cod liver oil or other fatty fish oil is a simple method to boost your pet's vitamin D levels.

Symptoms of a lack of vitamin D can be seen in the hamster's hips and walking gait. If your pet isn't getting enough vitamin D, its bones will lose calcium and become deformed or fragile. This is most visible in your pet's hips and will affect its mobility. A word of warning: too much vitamin D in a hamster's diet can cause diarrhea and weight loss, so make sure any supplement you give to your pet is of the correct dosage.

- **Vitamin E** maintains the health of your hamster's skin and fur. Vegetables such as spinach and broccoli contain vitamin E. Sunflower seeds are also a good source of vitamin E but should be fed to your hamster sparingly (a few seeds per day).

Symptoms of a vitamin E deficiency include balding in patches, lameness, and muscle paralysis. However, too much vitamin E can cause diarrhea and weight loss.

Some pet shops offer a premixed concoction of vitamins for hamsters. Some products are in liquid form to be mixed into the water in the hamster's bottle or food, and others are given directly.

Some owners report their elderly hamster gaining a new lease on life and improved sleeping habits with the addition of supplements in its diet, so this might be helpful if your hamster's new routine is starting to interfere with your sleep (elderly hamsters, like elderly humans, can become early risers!).

Changes in Behavior

> "
>
> *Often when hamsters get older, they sleep a lot more, and you don't see them as often, but we don't encourage people to bother them and try to force them to interact. They will often stop using their wheel or will walk on it instead of running like they did when they were younger. Many older hamsters will no longer climb as much, so we give them lots of space on the ground level to burrow or make themselves a nice nest.*
>
> CINDY CRIBBS
> *Haven for Hamsters Rescue & Sanctuary*
>
> "

It's not unusual for your pet hamster's personality to change as it ages. Your hamster may have pain, and this can cause your pet to be more irritable, snippier, and perhaps less playful.

When you approach your hamster, allow it more time to sniff and identify you, as age may have affected its eyesight and memory. It might take a little longer before it feels comfortable being held. Hamsters sometimes become more vocal as they age, squeaking more frequently and for more reasons.

I've experienced elderly hamsters squeaking because they're in pain, because they're happy, and also because they're lost and are calling for

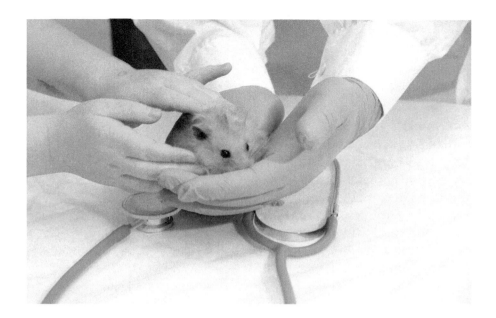

help. Use all your detective skills and your knowledge of your pet to try and work out what your hamster is trying to communicate.

Preparing for Your Hamster's Passing

It's inevitable that your hamster will pass away at some point. One day, you may find your pet curled up in its bed, appearing to be asleep, and you only realize it's dead when it doesn't respond to you. In this instance, you might not know the cause of death, but it's likely that your pet died of old age if it's two years of age or older and there was no evidence of illness.

Due to their small size, it can be difficult even for vets to properly diagnose a hamster, and available medicines are limited for such tiny animals. As your hamster ages, and especially if you feel it's close to passing, it's important that you spend quiet time with your pet and make it feel as comfortable as possible in its final days/weeks. Feed it treats, give it an extra stroke, and enjoy just being with your pet.

Euthanasia

If at any point you suspect that your hamster is in pain, it may be a good idea to bring it to your veterinarian with the intent of euthanizing it. It can be extremely difficult and stressful to determine when your hamster is struggling and in pain. It may sleep all day and barely move, and it may refuse food and water.

Photo Courtesy of Tiffany Booker

Euthanizing your hamster involves your hamster being put into a sealed container like a jar and the jar being filled with a gas used as anesthesia during surgery. In euthanasia, the vet overdoses the hamster with the gas. This will initially make your hamster feel drowsy and fall asleep. Then, as the concentration of gas increases, your hamster's oxygen level drops, and its heart and brain cease to function. Your hamster will feel no pain and won't be aware of what's happening.

Some vets will then inject a drug into the hamster's heart to ensure that the heart stops beating, and all vets will check with their stethoscope to make sure there's no heartbeat.

Grieving Your Loss

Our pets always take a chunk of our hearts with them when they die. It's completely normal for you to feel sad, lonely, or upset at the loss of your beloved pet.

If your hamster was euthanized, you can take its body home with you and have a proper burial. Otherwise, your pet will be cremated at a crematorium.

If you wish to bury your pet at home, find somewhere in your garden or yard where it can't be discovered and dug up by an animal and isn't in an area that might flood. Use a paper or cardboard box or wrap the body in tissue paper. Don't use a plastic container, as these don't disintegrate and are bad for the environment. Your vet can provide you with more information.

Regardless of whether you bury your pet or your vet handles its cremation, you can honor your hamster in several ways.

- Create a personalized burial ceremony in which you have the opportunity to say your goodbyes.
- Write down your feelings about losing your pet, and don't be afraid to share those feelings with friends and family.
- Take the time you need to grieve. It's okay to feel sad.

Resist the urge to immediately go out and buy another pet. You might make a bad decision based on your emotions.

CONCLUSION

Photo Courtesy of Molly Abrahams

Having a hamster as a friend and companion can be a heartwarming experience for both you and your pet. With patience, time, and attention, you can develop a trusting and loving relationship with your furry friend.

Before purchasing a hamster, think about the reasons you want to have one. Is it the right animal for you? Do you have the time to provide love and care? Choosing the right species of hamster for you will come down to what sort of space you have for a habitat, how much time you have to devote to your hamster, and if you're okay with a pet that might prefer to be observed rather than handled. Syrian hamsters are the friendliest, and their size and personality are better suited to younger owners. Smaller breeds of hamsters are better suited to older owners who understand the personality traits of these breeds. The benefit of Dwarf varieties is that you can often keep more than one of them together in a habitat, so they're less likely to get lonely. This can benefit an owner who has less time to play with them.

A hamster is a pet that can belong completely to you and is your responsibility. If you take good care of your hamster and give it lots of attention, it will reward you with a friendship you'll never forget. You'll learn so much about yourself and your pet along the way, and you'll create moments to treasure.

If you're unsure about whether a hamster is the right pet for you or you have general questions about its care, there are many people who own and breed hamsters and are willing to help you with any questions or issues you have.

Ultimately, trust your instincts as your knowledge of and relationship with your hamster develops. You know your pet best, and your hamster will make it known to you if anything isn't quite right or if it's unhappy.

While your time with your hamster may feel like a fleeting moment in your long life, remember that you'll be there for all your pet's time on earth. You're its daily companion, its friend, and its caregiver, and your pet completely relies on you for its health and well-being.

Printed in Great Britain
by Amazon

48416468R00056